John Dewey and Education Outdoors

John Dewey and Education Outdoors

Making Sense of the 'Educational Situation' through more than a Century of Progressive Reforms

John Quay
The University of Melbourne, Australia

and

Jayson Seaman
University of New Hampshire, USA

SENSE PUBLISHERS
ROTTERDAM/BOSTON/TAIPEI

A C.I.P. record for this book is available from the Library of Congress.

ISBN: 978-94-6209-213-6 (paperback)
ISBN: 978-94-6209-214-3 (hardback)
ISBN: 978-94-6209-215-0 (e-book)

Published by: Sense Publishers,
P.O. Box 21858,
3001 AW Rotterdam,
The Netherlands
https://www.sensepublishers.com/

Printed on acid-free paper

TABLE OF CONTENTS

ILLUSTRATIONS

ACKNOWLEDGEMENTS

Collaborating on a book from different sides of the world has not been a simple undertaking, yet both of us have enjoyed immensely the intellectual stimulation and the challenge of working through our differing perspectives that have been features of such a process. The end product fulfils the old cliché of being much more than a sum of the parts.

We initially planned to get together in a physical sense to do much of the thinking and discussing necessary for such a project; however, while these plans did not eventuate we were able to use many of the advancements in communication technology available to us to forge a successful writing relationship. In Dewey's day such an undertaking would perhaps have been much more daunting or at least more time consuming, but today we feel part of the mainstream of online communication.

A book written in this way requires the support of family, and both of us would like to warmly acknowledge the understanding of our wives and children who had to deal with the numerous face-to-face online meetings conducted at odd times – usually at early hours of the morning or in the evening – in order to overcome the time differences between our physical locations. These times of the day are busy family times when children are involved and there was always a lot going on in the background during our conversations.

We would also like to acknowledge the many, many people whose lives have been entwined with the histories that we unfold through this book. It was never our intention to provide an exhaustive account of all the many important twists and turns that make up such histories, so numerous important persons will not have been mentioned directly in our specific argument. This argument, supported by our interpretations of Dewey's work, is illuminated by particular historical developments in outdoor education, which necessarily have required some selection. Other developments may have been just as important, but escaped our gaze.

Finally, we would like to thank those who helped us in our search for the photographs that adorn the text, particularly Cliff Knapp, who shared photos from the era of school camping, Jim Garrett, who provided photos from early Outward Bound days, Arlene Ustin, who sourced archival photos of Kurt Hahn, and Deb Bialeschki, who facilitated access to early summer camp photos. These images put faces to some of the names and add insight to some of the initiatives that many of us have heard mentioned when reading and talking about outdoor education in its many guises.

FOREWORD

Be prepared to do some deep and reflective thinking as you read this book. You are about to probe a topic that is close to my heart. I have spent more than 50 years teaching people of all ages about the importance of learning outside the four walls of the classroom and school. Of course, I have taught inside classrooms and schools too, but my focus has been to investigate the knowledge gained by extending education into the community and beyond.The authors of this book have done their homework and written about a field of study labeled 'outdoor education' and how different people, including the philosopher/educator John Dewey, have interpreted the meaning of that and related terms. They hope to give you a better understanding of how learning outside classrooms has changed over the years and what may lie ahead in the future. Fortunately, I have met many of the people quoted in this book, so I had a nostalgic journey throughout the pages.

You may be thinking that there is nothing new or surprising about this kind of teaching, and that you've known it as an excursion or field trip away from the school. If you were lucky, your teacher took you outside the classroom in elementary, middle or high school, and even in college, and when you think back over these experiences, you may still remember some of what you learned when you left the classroom. This is because these activities are designed to reinforce concepts, skills, and values through direct experiences in local contexts and to actively engage students so that they are motivated to learn and retain what is required in the curriculum. In order to communicate this way of reforming education to others, educators decided to describe it by placing the adjective, 'outdoor' (meaning outside the classroom) as a prefix to the word 'education.' As time passed, different words have been used to describe the 'how' and 'what' of this type of school reform: nature education, camping education, conservation education, environmental education, adventure education, experiential education, earth education, bioregional education, ecological education, place-based education, and more. I have compiled an ever-expanding list of terms, currently at 78, that have been used to label these fields of study designed to reform education by expanding the concept of 'classroom.'

As you will read, schools were not the only institutions to initiate programs of learning in the local or surrounding areas. Recreational facilities such as parks and nature centers joined the movement into the outdoors. Scouting, YMCAs, 4-H, and other service groups and hospital therapeutic programs sometimes took advantage of special environments to promote their goals. Also, Outward Bound, National Outdoor Leadership Schools, and wilderness educators started programs of outdoor adventure using canoes, kayaks, and backpacks. Because diverse groups with various goals and objectives adopted the term, 'outdoor education', confusion sometimes arose about what the term meant.

On October 15, 1859 Henry David Thoreau, a leading spokesperson for nature education in America, wrote in one of his journals:

> We boast of our system of education, but why stop at schoolmasters and schoolhouses? We are all schoolmasters, and our schoolhouse is the universe. To attend chiefly to the desk or schoolhouse while we neglect the scenery in which it is placed is absurd. (Thoreau, 2001, p. 500)

John Dewey, renowned as a leader in the Progressive Education Movement in the United States and abroad, also promoted the idea of outdoor education in a film produced by the March of Time in 1937. The film, *Youth in Camps: Life's Summer Camps*, showed how L. B. Sharp wanted to reform camping education. Dewey (as cited in Sharp & Osborne, 1940, p. 236) said:

> The average American child seldom comes in direct contact with nature. In school he learns a few dates from books, to press a button, to step on an accelerator; but he is in danger of losing contact with primitive realities – with the world, with the space about us, with fields, with rivers, with the problems of getting shelter and of obtaining food that have always conditioned life and that still do.

He also wrote:

> The teacher should become intimately acquainted with the conditions of the local community, physical, historical, economic, occupational, etc., in order to utilize them as educational resources. (Dewey, 1938, p. 40)

The fact that early educators taught lessons mostly confined to inside classrooms, prompted a growing interest in opening the school door and going outside to learn some of the required subject matter when it made pedagogical sense. Thoreau's and Dewey's directives were not always followed in the ensuing years and therefore outdoor education, in its varied forms, was introduced into the curriculum under different labels. The criticism that many educators today limit their teaching to the indoor classroom prompts repeated attempts at school reform. Some contemporary educators believe that youth are alienated and separated from many essential outdoor experiences and that they need outdoor education more today than ever.

Perhaps the time will soon arrive when educators will drop the many prefixes, (such as outdoor, environmental, nature, adventure, and experiential), to describe the type of education they think is important for youth. Maybe the only prefixes that will be used will be 'good' or 'effective' and we can close the book on confusing meanings of other educational terms. I wonder if I'm too much of a dreamer and idealist to ever see that come about? Now you are ready to delve into the story of how John Dewey and other educators influenced the idea of learning in the broader classroom known as the community and surrounding open spaces.

Clifford E. Knapp, Professor Emeritus
Department of Teaching and Learning, Northern Illinois University
DeKalb, Illinois, U. S. A.

WHY BE CONCERNED WITH OUTDOOR EDUCATION?

Although garnering attention most recently due to the identification of "nature deficit disorder" in the early 21st century (Louv, 2008; see also Cooper, 2005), concern for children's contact with nature has actually influenced education for many years. In response to these concerns, various forms of so-called 'outdoor education' have appeared throughout the 20th century. Looking back, one can now see that outdoor education functions like other reform monikers – as a seemingly simple label that actually carries a range of meanings, and is often mobilized by different reformers to achieve different purposes. Some may view unpacking these meanings as a mere semantic exercise, but, in the world of educational reform, labels and their meanings are more than that: in practice they represent a range of educational values and priorities that sometimes overlap but can also contradict one another. Practitioners and scholars alike should therefore be alert to seemingly consensual terms that mask cultural conflicts and historical changes, as outdoor education has done for over a century now. We believe that scrutinizing how the term outdoor education has operated over time is more than an exercise in semantics; it can help uncover some of the deepest and most longstanding problems with education itself.

On its face, the term outdoor education doesn't sound any alarms – what could be more natural than children learning in the outdoors? As we will show, however, fierce controversies have arisen over the term – including the significance of hyphens as with the term *nature-study*! The first decade of the 21st century has seen a resurgence in calls for more contact with the outdoors both in and out of schools, some even reaching crisis proportions (Mueller, 2009). But these calls echo prior movements and can benefit from a critical look at what the term outdoor education has meant throughout the past century.

Given the variations in meaning over time, such a look will require attending to what John Dewey (1931, p. 1) called "educational confusion." Outdoor education has a history as long as institutionalized schooling itself and it therefore provides a compelling case study of how reform movements typically follow cycles as they introduce exciting new practices but ultimately tend to succumb to the forces they were meant to overthrow. To be clear, we are not suggesting that reformers themselves were confused in the sense of being disoriented and vague about what they were trying to accomplish. Indeed, as we will show, like Dewey's contemporaries they often argued very forcefully and precisely about what outdoor education ought to involve.

If we do not intend confusion to mean the mental state of specific reformers and their allies, how do we mean it? We use it throughout the book as Dewey himself did: as a way to characterize the contradictions and paradoxes that recur within the seemingly never-ending debates about proper educational priorities and approaches – including the desire to get children outdoors more regularly. A main issue that preoccupied Dewey over many years, and the one we take up in this book, is the persistent dichotomy between *method* and *subject matter*, or as Dewey famously put it, *child* and *curriculum*. So, while specific outdoor education reformers were often very clear about their own meanings and the programs they wanted to see implemented, one can see in retrospect that the larger debates in which they were embroiled bear the tell-tale marks of this dichotomy. Through a Deweyan lens, one can read these recurring debates as an indication of a more pervasive confusion about what education fundamentally *is*. As Dewey wrote in 1900, already the tendency was to emphasize technical details and lose sight of the broader societal function of education – to miss the forest because one is focusing on the trees, so to speak:

> Whenever we have in mind the discussion of a new movement in education, it is especially necessary to take the broader, or social view. Otherwise, changes in the school institution and tradition will be looked at as the arbitrary inventions of particular teachers; at the worst transitory fads, and at the best merely improvements in certain details. (Dewey, 1900, p. 20)

Although it was not his intent, we believe Dewey does a fair job here of forecasting the next century of outdoor education reforms (among many others – see Kliebard, 2004 for an excellent overview of the history of school reform). Rather than fundamentally changing education, reforms can get caught in dichotomous ways of thinking that wind up reproducing the dominant structures of institutionalized schooling that marginalize important initiatives like outdoor education. In other words, because the larger educational conversation is itself confused, reforms such as outdoor education that engage on its terms often contain the seeds of their own undoing right from the start.

Although its advocates might like to believe that outdoor education is somehow special, its history evidences what educational historians David Tyack and Larry Cuban have called "tinkering toward utopia" (1995) – their name for the process by which innovative and sweeping reforms become absorbed by schools, improving conditions for specific children for a time but ultimately changing the overall shape of the institution ever so slightly if at all. But we do believe outdoor education is somewhat unique in its history of tinkering and therefore deserves special attention. Because it has always straddled the boundary between classroom-based and out-of-school learning, it provides a compelling test case for closely examining and then moving past the educational confusion that bedevilled Dewey.

On the surface this is a book about outdoor education, an array of compelling progressive reforms whose history has yet to be satisfactorily written, its pioneers and trendsetters unrecognized side by side in one volume. Practitioners and scholars of outdoor education should therefore find this aspect of the book valuable.

Beyond that though, the deeper purpose of the book is to provide a framework for thinking about curriculum theory that does not reproduce the problems inherent in prevailing ways of thinking – in which the method/subject matter dichotomy usually, but often subtly, dominates.

To tack back and forth between the specifics of outdoor education and this broader theoretical concern, we use three devices that we want to make obvious to readers at the outset: (1) providing a historical narrative of outdoor education in the USA, in which we profile prominent reformers and the programs/ideas they represented; (2) tracking explicitly how this history has operated in a series of cycles in which similar issues and themes arise; and (3) invoking John Dewey throughout and especially at the end, where we elaborate on his theories where the "social view" (1900, p. 20) is made central to education. A brief word on each of these will help orient readers to the rest of the book.

The unfolding story of outdoor education from early beginnings in the 1800s provides the core of the book which journeys from its initial form in what came to be called nature-study, to a present which embraces what Clifford Knapp described in 1997 as "a list of more than 50 terms that fit under the umbrella describing our field" (p. 4).

> When I began my career, we used only a handful of terms: outdoor education, school camping, conservation education, nature study, nature recreation, and outdoor recreation, to mention a few. Now we have added many more including: earth education, ecological education, energy education, expeditionary learning, environmental and environment education, adventure and challenge education, outdoor ethics education, bioregional education, science-technology-society education, global environmental change education, and sustainable development education. Just look in any professional conference program for some of these terms and for the variety of activities offered. (Knapp, 1997, p. 4)

How can one term refer to so many values and programs? Wouldn't they sometimes come into conflict with each other, while in other cases echoing one another? The answer is yes, and these echoes and conflicts provide telling insights into the ways school reforms reflect broader cultural priorities. But what is also revealing is the way in which these specific reforms have interacted and supplanted one another over time, a pattern that is only discernable once one moves beyond the seemingly homogeneous term 'outdoor education.'

Our historical narrative will therefore reveal that the process of introducing new forms of outdoor education has occurred in a cyclical fashion. This is the second structural feature of the book we want to point out to readers. The cycle we identify is one of ongoing curricular reform, where anxiety among teachers, itself driven by children's dissatisfaction in schools, leads to the introduction of educational initiatives that could be described as *student-centered*. This, for instance, is how nature-study initially developed (in tandem with nostalgic concerns over a declining agricultural economy). The cycle works roughly like this: initiatives like nature-study become gradually more popular among teachers and students as word spreads of their seeming ability to capture students' attention because of their emphasis on the *child*. But rather than remaining satisfied with student centeredness, ultimately some people start to voice concerns about the role of subject matter in these new initiatives. When this happens, subject matter or *curriculum* content can become the focus, gradually shifting the character of the original initiative and rendering it open to becoming a 'regular' school subject. In this vein, nature-study – as one example – very easily morphed into school science, and then even more specialized subjects such as botany.

Once the outdoors can be studied indoors in the form of science, children start to spend more time in classrooms and again become disenchanted with school. This creates a need for new educational initiatives to fill the void that has been reopened. Yet another 'new' student-centered initiative gradually takes shape, usually with a new name. As this nascent initiative gains significant traction, it slowly but surely falls victim to the same forces; the cycle starts again. And the invariable result is that outdoor programs, rather than being coherently and systematically incorporated into education, become isolated and jostle for position in an already 'crowded curriculum.' This trend was already being recognized as widespread by reformers in the late 1800s (e.g., Dewey, 1896; Rice, 1888; Strong, 1889), well before outdoor education had proliferated in the way Cliff Knapp describes.

When one becomes aware of this cyclical movement, unfolding over extended periods of time and usually resulting in 'crowding' rather than fundamental reform, it begs the question: 'Why does this keep happening?' To try and answer this question we developed what is the third important structural feature of this book: an analysis based on the educational philosophy of John Dewey. Here Dewey's awareness of educational confusion – and, more importantly, his admittedly complicated attempts to end it – guide us in presenting a case for understanding why this cycle exists, and also how we might move beyond it by reimagining the relationships between core concepts. And although we focus on outdoor education *per se*, we believe Dewey's lessons apply to education more generally.

JUST WHAT *IS* OUTDOOR EDUCATION?

A CONFUSED EDUCATIONAL SITUATION

In the USA, the specific term *outdoor education* began to be used as early as the first decade of the 1900s (Curtis, 1909). At this time outdoor education simply meant a form of education that wasn't indoor education. Reformers used the terms *out-door*, or *out-of-doors*: hyphenated terms communicating a sense of being active in settings other than classrooms. To be involved in out-door education one had to exit a literal door into the school yard, the school garden, the community past the school fence, and perhaps even the woods beyond.

The juxtaposition between education conducted in-doors and out-doors, indoor education and outdoor education, defined outdoor education early on, and it made sense – if one accepted the idea that the two distinct forms of education could, or should, be marked off from one another. School-based education was primarily conducted indoors, the literal door also marking a figurative boundary between two different worlds, one more real to young people because it connected directly with life beyond school, the other connected to their lives only remotely.

This was the educational situation that Dewey encountered at the turn of the 20th century, where 'outdoor education' for many children still involved learning through firsthand work in agricultural trades (see 1902a), and as reformers tried to implement programs that leveraged these familiar practices. He observed and wrote about this in his small text titled *The Educational Situation*. Such a distinction, then characterized by indoor and outdoor education, indicated to Dewey a broader and more deeply conflicted and confused educational situation. But rather than seeing the conflicts between these two forms of education as indicative of two truly different 'educations' – as his contemporaries argued – he described their interplay as a historical condition of the "the wave by which a new study is introduced into the curriculum" (p. 14). This was a time when school was overtaking traditional community activities as the main site for children's learning on a mass scale, and when new initiatives, some of which would eventually be labelled outdoor education, were entering schools as part of an enthusiastic wave of reforms:

Someone feels that the school system of his[1] town is falling behind the times. There are rumors of great progress in education making elsewhere. Something new and important has been introduced; education is being revolutionized by it; the school superintendent, or members of the board of education, become somewhat uneasy; the matter is taken up by individuals and clubs; pressure is brought to bear on the managers of the school system; letters are written to the newspapers; the editor himself is appealed to to use his great power to advance the cause of progress; editorials appear; finally the school board ordains that on and after a certain date the particular new branch – be it nature study, industrial drawing, cooking, manual training, or whatever – shall be taught in the public schools. The victory is won, and everybody – unless it be some already overburdened and distracted teacher – congratulates everybody else that such advanced steps are being taken. (Dewey, 1902a, pp. 14–15)

But this was never the end of the story, for "the next year, or possibly the next month, there comes an outcry that children do not write or spell or figure as well as they used to" (Dewey, 1902a, p. 15). And more than this, "that they cannot do the necessary work in the upper grades, or in the high school, because of the lack of ready command of the necessary tools of study" (p. 15).

We are told that they are not prepared for business, because their spelling is so poor, their work in addition and multiplication so slow and inaccurate, their handwriting so fearfully and wonderfully made. Some zealous soul on the school board takes up *this* matter; the newspapers are again heard from; investigations are set on foot; and the edict goes forth that there must be more drill in the fundamentals of writing, spelling, and number. (Dewey, 1902a, p. 15)

While Dewey's simplified tale is more than a century old, his message about confusion – in which 'traditional' and 'progressive' reformers push and pull, and programs wax and wane – still rings true today. Then, Dewey (1902a, p. 20) attempted to cut through the confusion by asking a provocative question: "Why do the newer studies, drawing, music, nature study, manual training; and the older studies, the three R's, practically conflict with, instead of reinforcing, one another?" Dewey deliberately represented the conflict in education as chiefly involving two sides, calling them "sects" or "schools of opinion" (1902b, p. 4). "One school fixes its attention upon the importance of the subject matter of the curriculum as compared with the contents of the child's own experience" (p. 7). While for "the other sect ... the child is the starting point, the center and the end" (p. 9). Therefore the child's development and growth "is the ideal. It alone furnishes the standard. To the growth of the child all studies are subservient; they are instruments valued as the serve the needs of growth" (p. 9). In shorthand Dewey described this as "the case of the child *vs.* the curriculum" (p. 5). Expressed in another way, this is the confusion in education between method and subject matter, where "method is ultimately reducible to the question of the order of development of the child's powers and interests" (1897a, p. 79); and "curriculum" is the "subject-matter of instruction" (1897b, p. 356). In Dewey's analysis, which he elaborated throughout his decades-long career, most of the educational confusion he observed stemmed from this persistent dualism, which most reformers neglected to question and therefore tacitly maintained.

Importantly, Dewey did not limit his analysis to schooling; he was, after all, a philosopher chiefly interested in education as a historical and cultural force and not as a technical matter of getting children to internalize a greater volume of content,

*Figure 1. John Dewey in 1902 (photo by Eva Watson Schutze
[public domain] courtesy of Wikipedia Commons).*

or learn it more effectively. He argued that the method/subject matter distinction could be traced to how people described the most basic aspects of human existence. He maintained that "reflection upon experience gives rise to a distinction of *what* we experience (the experienc*ed*) and the experienc*ing* – the *how*" (1916, p. 196). And "when we give names to this distinction we have subject matter and method as our terms" (p. 196). In other words, assuming an actual distinction between subject matter and method was a philosophical mistake stemming from a misunderstanding about lived experience and its relation to reflective thinking.

This mistake influenced how most people thought about education and it shaped reform debates of Dewey's day. Too often, educational reformers based their conceptions and thus their initiatives on this mistake and not the basic existential condition *within* experience – that subject matter and method are unified, or, in Dewey's language, they are "continuous" (1916a, p. 196; see also 1938). Throughout his career Dewey was vexed by this mistake, which he referred to as a false conflict between new and old, progress and tradition, method and subject matter, how and what, and child and curriculum. Figure two illustrates the usual way of conceiving of 'sides' of this debate as it is played out in education.

This division also points into the heart of how outdoor education has evolved over the century since Dewey first discussed it, and is evident today in terms such as student-centered vs. teacher-centered, process vs. content, pedagogy vs. curriculum, constructivist vs. didactic teaching, and emergent vs. standardized curricula. The persistence of these debates or even the occasional victory of one side over the other suggest that reformers have not significantly moved past the confusion Dewey wrote about as early as the 1890s, failing to develop a more holistic and comprehensive understanding of education.

Our central argument in this book is that the persistent conflicts (what we will henceforth call *confusion,* as Dewey meant it) created by struggles over this

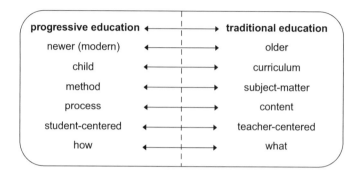

Figure 2. The two sides Dewey saw involved in educational conflict, confusion and compromise.

differentiation between method and subject matter, can be seen in the evolution of outdoor education in the USA, where advocates have vacillated between questions such as 'Is it a unique method?' or 'Is it a distinctive content area?' Debates over these questions have raged for a century. In a Deweyan sense outdoor education suffers from the same confusion as other reforms; it will likely remain so until advocates move beyond the dualism Dewey tried so hard to abolish.

FROM OUT-OF-DOORS TO ENVIRONMENT TO PLACE

When outdoor education first emerged as an educational term and movement in the early 1900s, its contribution was primarily on the child side of Dewey's distinction, as a new method that better tapped into children's natural interests and enabling traditional areas of subject matter to be encountered in more engaging ways. Predecessors to this version of outdoor education included nature-study, school gardens, and agricultural education. Camping also came to be considered outdoor education, leading to the spread of school camping in the mid-20th century. But in all of these new offerings the main emphasis remained on *method* – getting outside enabled a different way of teaching; this was the point. No major claims were made about curriculum, thus there was no apparent confusion. The educational situation of which Dewey wrote had not yet become a significant issue for most outdoor educators, who were mainly concerned with offering an alternative to staid, classroom instruction. Thus the distinction was often portrayed as a positive one by progressive educators who highlighted the problems with indoor education and schooling in general.

Various questions were, however, raised about the role of subject matter even in the earliest forms of outdoor education, starting with nature-study. The result was a continual process of adding new educational offerings that prioritized *method*, many of which then made a steady migration to the other side of the equation because they introduced new possibilities for *subject matter* – which of course had to find a place amidst already existing topics. This contributed to the growing problem of the "crowded curriculum" (Dewey, 1896, p. 9), a problem that most readers will recognize within schools today.

The first historical details of this spiral-like process are outlined in chapter two, which runs from the early 1830s with nature-study (although at this time the actual term *nature-study* had not yet appeared) to the 1960s. But of course the reform cycle is observable up to the present. In chapter three we cover the 1960s to the 2000s. It is at the junction of these two chapters, however, in the 1960s, that confusion about the meaning of the term outdoor education really begins to compound. Prior to this time, agreeing upon a definition for outdoor education amongst those involved was not particularly pressing, although attempts were definitely made. But as more scholarly articles and books began to appear and as other reforms competed for prized space in the curriculum, the need to claim a definitive answer to the question 'What is outdoor education?' became more urgent.

The 1960s was therefore something of a watershed decade for outdoor education as its varieties proliferated. Growing concern for the health of the environment began to influence public discourse and outdoor education was not immune to these forces. In fact, outdoor education was seen by many as an ideal educational response to environmental issues. The heightened focus on the environment brought with it a subtle but powerful shift in understandings of the term *outdoor* as applied in outdoor education. From its beginnings as a new method of education that advocated for *being out-of-doors* as opposed to indoors, outdoor education was developing into an area of education concerned mainly with *the environment* (primarily the natural environment), and this concern heightened the focus on subject matter in addition to the existing emphasis on method.

With the cultural focus on the environment gaining momentum through the 1960s (leading, for example, to the first Earth Day in 1970), talk turned to conservation education and environmental education. *Outdoor education* emerged as a prominent and possibly overarching label among the array of educational responses to the environmental crisis. The increasing meaning for the outdoors as *environment* raised the possibility that knowledge about the environment could be the main subject matter for outdoor education, which meant it could finally be recognized as distinct and legitimate. Some, including Phyllis Ford (1981), argued that this academic domain should be called outdoor/environmental education. None of this debate, however, was new; just as nature-study had steadily become botany and other specialized sciences, outdoor education was becoming a subject area focused on ecological understandings.

Thus the reform wave Dewey wrote about had an ebb as well as a flow. Yet again, a new progressive initiative that was introduced as a way to appeal to young people's interests became transformed into traditional disciplines as subject matter was distilled and codified as important knowledge about nature. This pattern is most evident with nature-study and again with environmental education in the 1960s. But while all this was occurring, others began to focus again on outdoor education as method.

Hence we also see in the 1960s a delineation from environmental and conservation education the new terms *experiential education* and *adventure education*, which – as we will show – were, in Dewey's terms, chiefly directed toward the child. Thus the question 'What is outdoor education?' became even more confused in the 1960s, starting yet another cycle and representing, but not reconciling, both sides of the method/subject matter dichotomy.

Adventure educator Simon Priest (1986) attempted to quell the confusion among these various areas by positioning outdoor education as an umbrella term (as it had been originally), but this time proposing two branches: environmental education and adventure education. These then split into four possible areas of relationship: ecosystemic (environment), ekistic (people-environment), interpersonal (people-people), intrapersonal (self). Environmental education, Priest argued, was primarily concerned with ecosystemic and ekistic relationships; adventure education dealt more with interpersonal and intrapersonal relationships.

Although it was an orderly and useful attempt, Priest's framework did not end the confusion. It instead cemented method and subject matter as distinct categories. Priest's concept of *relation* was intended to be the connecting link, but the different forms of relation were now cast as different forms of education: environmental education focused more on relations between person and subject matter (i.e., knowledge of and attitudes toward nature), and adventure education focused on interpersonal relations, without specification of any crucial subject matter or curricular sequence. There appeared to be some hope that environmental education would more explicitly embrace experiential – i.e., constructivist, learner-centered – methods, however, because of the necessary commitment to subject matter, the methods often embraced within environmental education involved field work that recapitulated existing scientific ideas, such as testing a fact or theory, as would a science experiment in a classroom or laboratory.

An emerging conceptual and practical way forward beyond this confusion between method and subject matter in outdoor education has gained popularity since Priest's proposal: place-based education. Author David Gruenewald (2005) claims that place-based education is not simply a method, that it also contains subject matter concerning the notion of place itself, which should be interpreted broadly. Gruenewald, however, is also very aware that place-based education has yet to be widely incorporated into more traditional forms of education, suggesting it is at the start of the method/subject matter cycle, and could experience the ebb towards institutionalization as subject matter curriculum. Will it escape the seemingly inevitable confusion? Time will tell, and the analysis we present throughout this book should provide a useful tool for making such forecasts and imagining ways forward.

SUMMARY

In this chapter, we have argued that outdoor education can be characterized as 'confused' in the sense that Dewey used this word, meaning it has vacillated between the two poles of method and subject matter, occasionally trying to overcome, but ultimately reproducing this dualism. The persistence of this confusion results in predictable reform cycles, sometimes starting out as new methods for engaging children but eventually being asked to specify and serve subject matter goals as they expand and become institutionalized – a phenomenon which usually distorts the original methods. This is not the fault of ill-intended or incompetent reformers, but rather, in our Deweyan view, a dynamic that stems from the pervasiveness of educational confusion more generally. This further indicates that outdoor education, no matter how far away from the classroom it gets, is subject to the powerful forces that shape school reforms – dynamics that Dewey spent his career trying to change.

If this situation has been around for many decades, are reformers simply resigning themselves to its continuation as they strive to create new forms of outdoor education in the 21st century? For much of his life Dewey was intent on overcoming this confusion. He even presented a lecture at Harvard University entitled *The Way Out of Educational Confusion* (Dewey, 1931), which, despite its pointed title, unfortunately did not settle the issue in the broader education landscape. Nonetheless, we believe that the core of Dewey's pedagogical argument, which has not seriously been considered in the outdoor education literature, offers a potential way through the confusion.

In the remainder of the book, we carry on with Dewey's project and use outdoor education as a kind of case example of (a) how persistent educational confusion is evident in reforms that attempt to overcome it, and (b) a compelling arena where an alternative and non-dualistic – or if you like, a 'non-confused' – pathway forward can be imagined. In the next two chapters, we provide a more substantial outline of the history of outdoor education reforms, supporting our assertion that confusion reigns. In chapter five we propose a way of understanding Dewey's philosophical work in light of this problem. Much of this revolves around his concept of experience (which, significantly, he later redefined to mean *culture*) and particularly his sense of "education *through* occupations" (1916a, p. 361). We outline these concepts in considerable detail in chapter six after discussing Dewey's radical philosophical solution to the recurring method/subject matter problem.

NOTES

[1] As was standard practice in the period during which Dewey was writing, the use of the pronoun 'he' was accepted as referring to all people. We therefore retain the masculine pronoun in Dewey's original text, while in our own we also variously use 'she.'

OUTDOOR EDUCATION AND INDOOR EDUCATION

THE EMERGENCE OF 'OUTDOOR EDUCATION'

The term outdoor education appeared in the USA around a century ago, first emerging in discussions of *open-air* or *out-door* schools designed to improve the health of children suffering tuberculosis and other ailments. Yet this "movement for out-door education," as Elnora Whitman Curtis (1909, p. 169) described it, was seen even then to have broader potential. Expressing her thoughts in the language of the day, Curtis (p. 169) argued that "the present movement for the establishment of open-air schools while relating to sickly and backward children, merits serious consideration of educators, as pointing to possible changes in methods and curricula likely to be of practical benefit to all school children." Curtis characterized the advantages of an out-door education in ways that might be familiar to modern educators:

> The advantages of studying nature at first hand and of substituting live growing things for museum specimens or book descriptions, and of cultivating habits of observation, is apparent to every student of elementary education. The advantage, also, of substituting the natural activities of play and work for the more artificial physical exercises of the schoolroom is too obvious to need more than a passing mention. Less obvious but no less important is the subtle influence of forest and field upon the aesthetic and emotional nature of children usually ignored in discussions of educational questions. (Curtis, 1909, p. 188)

This early "outdoor school movement" (Upton, 1914, p. iii) that promoted "outdoor education" (p. 3) gained momentum. In so doing, it gradually brought together under one banner a range of educational practices that found common interest in moving beyond the confines of the classroom. In addition to open-air schools were the compatible areas of nature-study, school gardens, agricultural education, home credits (academic credit for work done at home), vacation schools, and others that stepped outside the classroom door (Zueblin, 1916). All of these would come to be called 'outdoor education.' For example, the monthly bulletin of the School Garden Association of America, whose first issue appeared in October, 1916, was called *Outdoor Education*. Notably prominent on the front cover of the first issue was a list of the educational endeavors meant to be associated with the term outdoor education: school gardens, home gardens, elementary agriculture, rural science, and nature-study.

The main unifying element in the different forms of so-called outdoor education was that they were not predominantly classroom-based. This common feature was evident in Charles Zueblin's (1916) use of the term "outdoor education" (p. 195) which he explicitly contrasted with the term "indoor education" (p. 177). Zueblin employed the outdoor-indoor distinction to structure his descriptions of the educational advances made in the USA at the time, establishing the superiority of those that occurred away from schoolhouse and classroom and thus, literally, out-of-doors. Zueblin characterized indoor education pejoratively as "the Gradgrind type of school, satirized by Dickens in 'Hard Times'" (p. 177). While he conceded that indoor education had been improved by progressive reforms, he maintained it was outdoor education that moved furthest from the classroom and its associated problems, both physically and symbolically:

> The hermetically sealed schoolhouse with rigid desks, inelastic curriculum, and impervious teacher is being rapidly supplanted by the open schoolhouse with movable furnishings and open-minded teacher. Light and air admitted freely are still not adequate for the freest education. City, as well as country, children must get into the open. Beginning with nature study in the classroom, nature has rapidly invited the school outdoors. (Zueblin, 1916, p. 195)

In referring to nature-study, Zueblin was bringing an already-established reform program in under the larger banner of 'outdoor education.' Of the various out-of-doors educational ventures Zueblin listed, the nature-study movement had already long offered a response to the problems perceived to exist with indoor, classroom-based education. Interestingly, even the term 'nature-study' was not uncontroversial within this movement. The term first appeared in 1880, but "the idea preceded the christening [with the term] by some years" (Comstock, 1915, p. 6). As the nature-study movement gained educational ground, the need to define the concept arose. Indicative of the controversy was a distinction grounded in the question: *Does it, or does it not, contain a hyphen?* "The group that supported not using the hyphen supported the position that nature study was primarily the study of nature" (Minton, 1980, p. iv). In contrast, "the opposition group believed that nature-study was more than the study of nature; it was a pedagogical idea with broad application in educational reform" (p. iv). As such "they felt that the use of the hyphen set the term apart and more clearly suggested their position" (p. iv).

The nature-study movement in the USA (readers should note the hyphen) occurred early in response to a perceived gap in the style of education that dominated American common schools, schools which were "a common feature of life in most American communities by 1830" providing "locally controlled, voluntary elementary schooling" (Kaestle, 1983, p. 62). The perceived gap in common school education did not primarily involve academic content, however. The emphasis in this early form of nature-study was children's interests, a focus at odds with much of educational practice at the time. In his review of the early development of nature-study in the USA, Ira Benton Meyers (1910, p. 209) recognized that the "pleasing and stimulating influence" of nature-study on children was amongst the main reasons for its introduction in the schools. This was circa 1830, "the period at which nature-study began to gain some headway in the common schools" (p. 207).[1] Recognizable even in this early period is debate surrounding the method/subject matter dichotomy; thus the seeds of confusion that would persist in outdoor education were already planted in the nature-study movement.

ORIGINS OF OUTDOOR EDUCATION IN NATURE-STUDY

The aim of the common schools during this early period "was to place the child in possession of the tools for acquiring knowledge and it was held that these tools were spelling, reading, writing, and arithmetic; along with some incidental training in behavior, morals, and religion" (Meyers, 1910, p. 207). Even Dewey (1900, p. 40) acknowledged that this was the period when "command of certain symbols, affording as they did the only access to learning, were all-important." According to John Swett (1900, p. 121), classrooms of this time were structured around the aim of "memorization of the textbook." Here "it was the office of the teacher to keep order and hear recitations"; at the same time "it was the duty of the pupils to memorize the textbook lessons and recite them without comment, or question" (p. 121). Indoor, classroom based education was primarily focused on memorizing content and this was reflected in the educational process.

Meyers (1910, p. 208) viewed Swett's description of classroom life as a fair representation of "the school atmosphere when nature-study entered." It was this Dickensian character of classroom life that stimulated the introduction of nature-study, which "did not enter as part of the system but as a thing aside" (p. 208). To be a part of the system was to emphasize the memorization of content and adhere to stifling classroom norms. Nature-study stood outside these norms and built instead on what Meyers described as the well recognized "instinctive interest of children in natural objects and phenomena," their "insatiable curiosity" and the "ease, wonder and delight with which they formed acquaintanceship with each new thing" (p. 208). All of this legitimated situating nature-study as a thing outside "real education," such that "the work was not looked upon as an *essential* part of school study." Rather nature-study "should be looked upon as a matter of recreation" (p. 209).

Today, what was then nature-study would be considered extra-curricular or co-curricular; it was definitively non-academic. And like today, the addition of recreational aspects to schooling was not accepted without complaint. Zueblin (1916, p. 180) noted that "opposition to the so-called 'fads' or 'frills' – nature-study, music, drawing, industrial and household arts – has been justified in part by their being superadded to a fixed system of education." In this practice of superadding one could see the tendency for what Dewey (1896, p. 9) called the "crowded curriculum," a now-routine problem which was already being discussed in the 1880s as a complication to the introduction of new subjects (see also Rice, 1888, Strong, 1889).

But significantly, superadding did not leave these new reforms unaltered. These 'fads and frills' were deeply affected by their addition to the system. Dewey observed these newer curricular offerings being transformed by the need to sequence courses of study across successive school grades. In doing so, he (1902b, p. 28) believed "the inevitable tendency is to arrest attention upon those parts of the subject-matter which lend themselves to external assignment and conjunction." In other words, the tendency was to see the importance of these new offerings mainly as a new form of content knowledge that could be subjected to ordered sequencing and external assessment:

> Even music, drawing and manual training are profoundly influenced by this fact. Their own vital aims and spirit are compromised, or even surrendered, to the necessities for laying out a course of study in such a manner that one year's work may fit externally into that of the next. Thus they part with much of their own distinctive and characteristic value, and become, to a considerable extent, simple additions to the number of routine studies carried by children and teacher. (Dewey, 1902b, pp. 28–29)

Even the early forms of nature-study would be incrementally absorbed within classroom-based education. From an auspicious origin in sincere concern for children's firsthand experience and interest – the raison d'être of the early versions of nature-study – the method was gradually transformed as it "got into the clutches of the system" (Meyers, 1910, p. 208). Ironically, a study that "took its initiative in the common schools because of what it promised in the way of wholesome physical, mental and religious training," by stressing "direct contact of children with their nature environment," eventually "ended in an attempt to teach an organized fund of knowledge for its own sake" (p. 212). And while this change did not immediately effect every school that offered nature-study, over a period of less than two decades nature-study was gradually subsumed within the system such that it became "wholly confined to botany" (p. 210), as a subject within indoor, classroom based education. Dewey (1902b, pp. 28–29) recognized that these studies could then be considered to "serve no new purpose of their own, but [rather they] add to the burden of the old." Thus "it is no wonder that when the burden gets too great there is demand that they be lopped off as excrescences upon the educational system" (p. 29).

Like Dewey, Meyers observed this spiral-like development proceeding through a series of stages:

> Its stages being: a recognition of the fact that children are instinctively interested in their nature environment; that their reactions to these interests exert on them a strong growth influence – physically, mentally, spiritually; the school attempts to utilize this interest; knowledge is systematized; a textbook is written, teachers are trained through a textbook, they attempt to teach children by the same method, contact with nature is lost, spontaneous interests vanish from the schoolroom, the study becomes a mere matter of memorizing the system, public protest, exit the study either by neglect or expulsion. (Meyers, 1910, p. 212)

Meyers prefaced his identification of these stages by commenting that they were not unique but were elements of a repeating cycle. "It will be of interest to note as we go on how frequently it has happened that a study, introduced into the schools for the purpose of ministering to the normal needs of children, has been turned about and used as an end instead of a means" (1910, pp. 211–212). Meyers (1911, p. 237) noticed that these stages had moved through their first cycle by the middle of the nineteenth century when botany had become a feature of the "higher schools ... because of its disciplinary value." Meanwhile, "in the elementary schools all organized attempts to teach natural history practically died out" (p. 237). Nature-study as a method concerned with captivating children's interests gave way to nature as an academic subject. Importantly, as nature-study of the 1830s moved indoors, the cycle began again. "By the early [eighteen] fifties a new movement was attempted and a strong plea made for a return to a freer out-of-door study of nature from the standpoint of the child's interests" (p. 237).

PROGRESS AND TRADITION IN NATURE-STUDY

Nature-study's cyclic evolution was not as straightforward the second time around. Meyers (1911, p. 238) observed that "this second movement for a return to nature from the standpoint of children's interests had made but little headway when it was intercepted." This 'interception' came in the form of "two ideas" (p. 238), one of which resulted in nature-study being conducted as "object-lessons" for the sake of improving children's analytical capacities, the other being the trend towards a general scientific understanding of nature. Gains made in the first reform wave of nature-study were not completely erased, but its progress became confounded by the added complexity of these dual emphases. Although well intended and at least initially concerned with bringing children into contact with nature beyond the classroom, both of these ideas eventually moved nature-study away from its connection with the interests of children and formalised it again as a subject area that could be taught indoors, using textbooks.

Systematizing nature-study: The expansion of object-lessons. Object-lessons were initially intended to engage children's interests, but they succumbed to the pressure to become more indoor and classroom based. "Object-lesson teaching had proved that the study of things could become as formal a process in learning as the textbook when things were not considered from the standpoint of the pupil's interests" (Meyers, 1911, pp. 240–241). Dewey also regarded object-lessons as problematic. "No number of object-lessons," especially when "got up as object-lessons for the sake of giving information, can afford even the shadow of a substitute for acquaintance with the plants and animals of the farm and garden acquired through actual living amongst them and caring for them" (1900, p. 24). Meyers (1911, p. 240) reported a similar situation with science, where "pupils analyzed, observed, dissected, not from any impulse of intense individual interest but because the laboratory manual so directed." And yet again, with all of this, "the complaint began again to grow that 'science and object-lessons as taught are becoming a grind and destroying children's instinctive interests in natural objects and phenomena'" (p. 240).

In less than a century, commentators had already observed two waves of 'nature-study' reforms and would soon witness a third. This one possessed a slightly different flavour than its predecessors due to an expanded effort to understand the child as a learner and to make deeper inroads into systemic change. The campaign for interests of the learner increased the demand upon teachers, who up to this point were apparently content to emphasize curricular content, to change their understanding of how education worked and thus the way they taught. In today's language, they were to become more learner-centered. The new focus on the pupil or child presented a difficult challenge for many traditionally oriented teachers. Compounding the strain on teachers grappling with this change was the hasty way in which nature-study was introduced into many schools. Dora Mitchell (1923, p. 305) reported the difficulties faced by teachers as "nature-study was introduced rapidly into state and city courses of study." The rapid pace of change magnified the significant challenge of grasping a new way of understanding education:

> Usually where nature-study was required, it was put into the curriculum by some one in authority and each teacher was notified to teach it. To many this order came as a distinct surprise. The subject had arisen in favor since they had their training. They were not imbued with the spirit of the movement and had vague ideas of its aim. Their own training had been formal, of the memorization type. The spirit of nature-study required of them new habits of thought, and their time was already fully occupied with numerous cares. As a consequence their teaching of nature-study was very perfunctory and unsatisfactory. (Mitchell, 1923, p. 305)

Dewey recognized the problems with this top-down administrative strategy. "To enact that at a given date all the grades of a certain city shall have nature study is to invite confusion and distraction" (1902b, p. 34). The issue for nature-study's advocates became how to communicate to practising teachers the nuances required by this shift in teaching practice, in a bureaucratic context characterized by administrative mandate. One solution: codify the new philosophy in some kind of teaching manual. As Meyers (1911, p. 242) pointed out, "up to this period (1891) the thing lacking to fuse this new work into one great movement was a good textbook or guide for teachers." Such a guide should emphasize the importance of an educational process or method based in the interests of the child in coming to understand the content, and it would function unlike traditional textbooks (which highlighted certain answers that would be supported by methods geared towards memorization). According to Meyers the most notable example of such a methods-oriented guide came in a publication by Wilbur Jackman (1891), who wrote a teaching manual specifically directed at teachers in the common schools.

Jackman's main purpose was to train teachers in a new way of teaching. He did not intend for his book to be simply a resource of factual information. Rather, he hoped that teachers would go so far as to engage with it in their own lives. He (1891, p. 26) believed that teachers could "never equip themselves for this work by reading alone," and he strove to assist teachers by "guiding them in their study so that they may acquire some of the necessary knowledge by actual work, and not with the intention of pouring out a mass of so-called facts for them to memorize." *Nature-Study for the Common Schools* was not a textbook but a guide for a teacher's own learning in the area of nature-study. Yet this point was missed by teachers who craved manuals that would provide facts: academic content they considered it their role to impart. Teachers "tried to do something but in many cases what they did was far from nature-study. Those that had had training in zoology and botany [simply] taught these subjects in diluted form" (Patterson, 1921, p. 56).[2]

Figure 3. Wilbur S. Jackman (photo [public domain] courtesy of Wikipedia Commons).

With laudable intentions, Jackman outlined a detailed process for how teachers could organize and conduct their nature-study teaching via insightful questioning based on firsthand observations. It offered a program that explicitly incorporated disciplines such as zoology, botany, geography and meteorology by focusing on the various natural cycles and events that occurred from season to season. But this shift to a focus on educational process and children's interests was too great a leap for many teachers. "The time for a book was never so ripe," Meyers (1911, pp. 242–243) recalled; "no book ever met so directly the spirit of the movement which it represented, and yet it proved a sore disappointment to teachers." Such disappointment stemmed from the fact that Jackman's book attempted to convey a method beyond the comprehension of many teachers, who had grown accustomed to teaching subject matter in a rote fashion.

Teachers still expected a curriculum consisting of answers, facts to communicate to pupils whose job it was to acquire them. Consequently, the book "met the teachers unprepared" (Meyers, 1911, p. 243). "It treated of outlook, of purpose, of methods of setting to work with the children, of what was best to do and how to do it" – essentially all those elements of process that supported the child in coming to meaningful terms with content – "but alas, it failed to tell the teacher what the results would be after she had done the work, it failed to give the answer to the questions asked." Jackman, himself, acknowledged that "as a mere 'Question and Answer Book,' this book must inevitably fail" (1891, p. 27). Meyers (1911, p. 243) captured the dominant perspective of teachers at the time by proclaiming that "it made little difference what the nature of the activity was, or the incentive under which carried on, it was *an* answer that was wanted." Content remained an antecedent collection of facts, with 'the teaching process' simply a matter of transmission.

Understanding nature-study's evolution. This tension in the late 1800s between science and nature-study, rooted in the division between subject-matter and method, was pinpointed by Liberty Hyde Bailey (1903) who analogously distinguished two types of teacher. "The teacher who thinks first of his subject teaches science; he who thinks of his pupil teaches nature-study" (p. 42). More forcefully he (p. 5) proclaimed that "nature-study is not science. It is not knowledge. It is not facts. It is spirit. It is concerned with the child's outlook on the world." Bailey's opinions on the teaching of nature-study were carried further by Anna Botsford Comstock, a colleague at Cornell University.[3]

> Nature-study is not elementary science as so taught, because its point of attack is not the same; error in this respect has caused many a teacher to abandon nature-study and many a pupil to hate it. In elementary science the work begins with the simplest animals and plants and progresses logically though to the highest forms; at least this is the method pursued in most universities and schools. The object of the study is to give the pupils an outlook over all the forms of life and their relation to one another. In nature-study the work begins with any plant or creature which chances to interest the pupil. It begins with the robin when it comes back to us in March, promising spring; or it begins with the maple leaf which flutters to the ground in all the beauty of its autumnal tints. A course in biological science leads to the comprehension of all kinds of life upon our globe. Nature-study is for the comprehension of the individual life of the bird, insect or plant that is nearest at hand. (Comstock, 1911, p. 5)

Comstock (1911, p. 1) believed that, "more than all, nature-study gives the child a sense of companionship with life out of doors and an abiding love of nature. Let this latter be the teacher's criterion for judging his or her work." But instituting such a major pedagogical shift through one area of study proved to be a difficult assignment. While many teacher training schools – what were then called 'normal' schools – introduced courses in nature-study in the early twentieth century, these courses were not a panacea either. In actuality they were generally "brief and afforded little opportunity for the mastery of the great variety of subjects touched upon by nature-study" (Mitchell, 1923, p. 312), not to mention the difficulties posed in trying to help teachers adopt a more child-centered process.

Figure 4. President Warren Harding with members of the nature-study class from the John Burroughs School looking at an owl's nest in a tree on the lawn of the White House, circa 1921 (photo courtesy of Library of Congress).

In spite of the challenges faced by nature-study's advocates, the desire for a more progressive form of education was beginning to gain acceptance in other areas. Dora Otis Mitchell (1923, p. 313) observed that "for at least two decades the leaders in nature-study were also the leaders in the progressive thought concerning elementary schools." But "within recent years many new ideals in other fields have come into progressive thought regarding elementary schools. The leadership in this thought has passed from the promoters of nature-study to others" (p. 314). Mitchell specifically identified an "emphasis on the practical" (p. 314) as an important outcome of these broader ideals: "Therefore it is held that in nature-study the child should be encouraged in his observation of those phenomena which have a practical bearing on his life" (p. 314). This was positively contrasted with an emphasis on observation as a purely academic task. As a result a new legitimacy was given to endeavours such as school gardening. Indeed, "the increased interest in school gardens illustrates this tendency to the practical" (p. 314 fn).

Amidst this growing diversity, nature-study was part of a wider set of progressive innovations that legitimized the move of teacher and pupils out-of-doors. As the School Gardening Association of America (1916) had highlighted, school gardens, home gardens, elementary agriculture and rural science were amongst a growing list of practical progressive alternatives which co-existed alongside nature-study as forms of outdoor education. However, while these various forms of outdoor education became more established features of school curricula in the USA in the early decades of the twentieth century, the conflict between the traditional

*Figure 5. School gardening at Jefferson School, Muskogee, Oklahoma, 1917
(photo courtesy of Library of Congress).*

emphasis on subject-matter (curriculum) and the more progressive focus on method (child) continued to percolate, resulting in further cyclical movements and a tendency to ignore more deep-rooted educational confusion. Those favoring content pulled nature-study and other forms of outdoor education towards the refined, disciplinary knowledge of science and its corresponding methods of classroom instruction, while those who emphasized process were concerned primarily with the interests and activities of children and strove to teach out-of-doors, academic subject-matter being important but only secondarily and within the context of firsthand activity.

FROM NATURE-STUDY TO NATURE LORE AND CAMPING

The difficulties in trying to shift the focus of nature-study away from subject matter to a child-centered method were taken up in a different way by Cap'n Bill Vinal, a movement pioneer who favored a more authentic, out-of-doors version of nature-study than usually undertaken in schools. He distinguished this version of nature-study by introducing the concept of nature-lore. "*Lore* is ... the sort of knowledge one gains by *experience*," he argued (1974–75, p. 3), identifying nature-lore more closely with the practicalities of everyday existence. Vinal (1940, p. vii) believed that "nature lore originated with the pioneer who loved his woodsy home. Through observation and experience, he built up a body of nature understanding and knowledge that both guided and enriched his existence." Therefore, "just as nature-study is not elementary science, – so too, nature-lore is not nature-study" (Vinal, 1922, p. 113). Vinal maintained that nature-lore achieved what many versions of school based nature-study could not, mainly because it was less constrained by the conventions of indoor education. This view led Vinal to favor camps as a more appropriate setting for outdoor education. "Schools cannot compete with camps as locations for the presenting of nature," wrote Vinal (1936, p. 463).

Figure 6. Cap'n Bill Vinal on a nature guiding walk with a group of teachers. Here they are looking at a pitcher plant from a quaking bog in New Jersey (photo courtesy of Clifford Knapp).

In an effort to establish a clearer distinction between nature-lore and nature-study, Vinal (1922, p. 113) provided "detailed comparisons" so as "to show the present differences in method and what we may expect as results." He made these comparisons in a series of points, quoted in full below:

1. nature-study is mainly aquaria, cages, flower pots, and pictures in the schoolroom, ... nature-lore is mainly swimming, fishing, foraging, and photographing out-of-doors;
2. nature-study is mainly studying living things or about living things ... nature-lore is mainly living with living things;
3. nature-study is mainly an outer urge ... it is a teacher made plan ... nature-lore is mainly an inner urge ... it is a self-assigned learning and is carried to a purposeful conclusion by the initiative of the learner;
4. nature-study in the traditional school is individualized ... the criticism is of the *method* of nature-study ... nature-lore in the summer camp and a few schools is socialized ... the summer camp is a small democracy;
5. nature-study is something that is taught ... nature-lore is something that is caught; and
6. nature-study starts and stops with a bell ... nature-lore comes at any time. (1922, pp. 114–116)

In short, Vinal perceived that nature-study had adopted a stronger content focus, while nature-lore was more oriented towards process and the interests of the child.

Figure 7. Cap'n Bill Vinal with campers inspecting the cutaway stump of a tree probably damaged by lightning (photo courtesy of Clifford Knapp).

For Bill Vinal, one crucial element of nature-lore was recreation, or more specifically, nature recreation. "Nature recreation is one of the greatest contributions that nature-lore can make to society," he (1926, p. 14) pronounced. Nature-lore required nature recreation, a form of recreation that occurred away from the classroom and in the out-of-doors, a position reminiscent of Meyers (1910, p. 209) characterization of the early nature-study as "a matter of recreation" in contrast to the "real education" carried on indoors. Vinal (1926, p. 15) noted that "nature-lore experiences come through such agencies as the summer camp and scouting organizations," which were also primarily recreational. "The fundamental movement of nature recreation to the out-of-doors had its inception in the *summer camp*," he (1940, p. viii) affirmed. While summer camps and scouting organizations were not schools, Vinal foresaw the possibility of a stronger interconnection between the two, a time when schools operated their own camps. Indeed, he (1922, p. 113) argued that the distinction he made between school based nature-study and camp oriented nature-lore could not be overcome "until the schools have their camps and their opportunities for forest recreation." Vinal was amongst the earliest champions of such integration:

> To emancipate children from schoolroom poison, to search for truth in the sunlight, and to declare independence of textbooks will require rethinking. To reshape our objectives so that the book will develop the individual instead of the subject of science, so that no one is "failed" but each has the opportunity to advance according to his own capabilities would seem drastic to some pedagogues. And yet for the past fifty years such a liberal policy has been used in camps. (Vinal, 1936, p. 463)

Organized summer camps for children (not school camps) had been slowly growing in popularity over the latter half of the nineteenth century in the USA, but it was in the early twentieth century that organized camping during summer vacation began to gain broad appeal. This was also a function of schooling. Ward (1935, p. 7) suggested that "probably the most distinctive reason why the summer camp should have originated in America" was the shape of the "American school calendar" with its extended break over summer. This calendar originated in farm life but became "fixed in custom" to the extent that "schools continued to close in the summer" (p. 7). Such a prolonged period of time with no school afforded an opportunity to better engage children's interests, with special concern directed toward urban youth. These concerns coincided with "the pioneer spirit and the vision of bringing back into our highly civilized and in many respects artificial method of living, those early values of life which come from living in the great out of doors" (Gibson, 1936, p. 13). Gibson emphasized what many at the time saw as a fundamental distinction between the goal of "out-doorness" as exemplary of a "cooperative way of living" and an opposing "in-doorness tendency" that reformers perceived to pervade the population in general.

Figure 8. Campers at the gate of YMCA Camp Dudley, the oldest continuously operating camp in the country, 1916 (photo courtesy of Camp Dudley YMCA Inc., Westport, New York).

THE RISE OF TRADITIONAL AND PROGRESSIVE CAMPING

As the popularity of organized summer camps grew, camping was itself shown to be susceptible to the same confusion between tradition and progress that afflicted the schools. In the camps the conflict revealed itself in the tension between the adult-designed camp program and the developing child. This tension escalated alongside the increase in the numbers of children and young people attending camps. Many camps reacted by simply getting bigger, and their programs became concomitantly more rigid and inflexible. In a report on the summer vacation activities of school children that emerged from a subcommittee of the White House Conference on Child

Health and Protection (1933, p. 40), chaired by William Heard Kilpatrick,[4] it was indicated that "the present tendency among camps is to increase in size. The camp of a hundred or more children is fast becoming the rule." The same report concluded that, in the main, "camp organization is so rigid and regimented, the child's day so routinized and scheduled that every moment of the day is provided for" (p. 39).

Figure 9. Campers involved in an official flag raising ceremony, 1924
(photo courtesy of Camp Namanu, Portland, Oregon).

While the burgeoning numbers indicated growth in opportunities for children and adolescents to access outdoor living, "the very growth in size of camps" had an institutionalizing effect on camp organization, which "tended toward more formal methods" (Ward, 1935, p. 40). Camping, which Carlos Ward (p. 39) described as initially "unfettered by schools, conventions and traditions," nonetheless was not immune from the same influences. His (p. 50) investigations revealed that "much of the same method of control and of stimulation to activity which we find in the grades and examination system of public schools" was being used in camps.

At the centre of these trends was the implementation of a fairly rigid system of "artificial and extrinsic incentives" in the form of awards, ranks or honors, similar to the scheme developed by scouting organizations, a system that, "while not military, had many elements which were capable of being treated almost as rigidly" (Ward, 1935, p. 42). The directors of summer camps "accepted this plan of points and awards because it served as an easy means of control and of keeping the campers busily occupied. It had not occurred to them that there might be some better way to do it" (p. 47). Ward (p. 42) suggested that these practices seemed "to have been taken along to camp as a matter of fact" because they were "common to the schools of that day."

Thus was transferred to out-of-school time and to activities not contemplated in school curricula much of the same method of control and of stimulation to activity which we find in the grades and examination system of public schools. It is true the course was broader and there were more electives, but the underlying philosophy and the principles of education were practically the same. (Ward, 1935, p. 50)

While for most of the early camps "the chief purpose was recreational and the great majority of camps have remained recreational" (Sargent, 1926, p. 27), this did not preclude many camps from adopting a traditional structure like that found in schools. The distinction between outdoor education and indoor education started to collapse as practices normally associated with traditional education were implemented in camps. Along with a focus on the curriculum and subject matter came corresponding methods of instruction; for example, the encroachment of rigid structures was exemplified in Ward's (1935, pp. 59–61) description of one camp where "intellectual," "physical," "service" and "devotional" were labels given to categories that were subject to a battery of tests. Camps adopted methods similar to those found in schools in order to more tightly manage their programs so as to control the larger numbers of campers. And because these methods were employed to manage all facets of camp life, the points and awards systems were, in effect, even more intrusive than similar systems used in schools. Virtually no part of camp life was devoid of points to be won, with awards used to affirm the smallest minutiae of everyday camp living. The apparent goal of many of these systems was a compliant camper, not unlike the school pupil in traditional education whose attitude must be "one of docility, receptivity, and obedience" (Dewey, 1938, p. 18).

Even summer camps that continued to pursue aims that were primarily recreational (rather than educational) subjected campers to the management methods used to control larger numbers of children. But, notably, these recreational camps did not trumpet any particular educational benefit from their programs. Some camp directors, however, sought to expand the educational possibilities of the summer camp – Bill Vinal among them. Hedley Dimock and Charles Hendry (1929, p. 1) observed "a shift in emphasis from a recreational to an educational function for the summer camp," accompanied by the conspicuous presence of "marked transformations in purpose, methods and leadership personnel." Such a profound shift occurred "in response to the newer currents which prevail in the field of educational theory and practice" (p. 1). Ward (1935, p. 156) identified this as a trend among "many camp directors ... to become progressive educationalists," and in so doing to be "more experimental and critical in their attitude to their work." These camp directors were more "ready to think things through in their own situations rather than follow time-worn traditions" (p. 156). Camps, in other words, increasingly became an arena of concern for those with an interest in progressive education.

Many of the people involved with camping, directors and counsellors included, were influenced to some degree by what they believed to be the basic tenets of progressive education, to the extent that *progressive camping* grew to be something of a term of art. Understandings of the concept of progressive camping, however, were not widely shared. "Progressive camping is a difficult conception in our authoritarian, mechanized and tradition bound world," Joshua Lieberman (1932, p. 9) pointed out. As it was for teachers in schools, the wholesale change required in educational thought in order to successfully move from traditional to progressive camping – that is, camping as a form of progressive education – was demanding of camp directors, many of whom did not have backgrounds in education. Nevertheless, this did not impede the rise in popularity of progressive camping, at least as a slogan. "Progressive camping not only is respected," Lieberman (p. 9) mused, "but has in some quarters become fashionable. As a result we have a drove of converts." But such popularity had its negatives as well as its positives. Lieberman (p. 9) played down the movement's apparent success, contending that "the 'victory' for progressive education is being too easily won. We have many verbal converts whose progressiveness consists largely of a new phraseology."

In his own practice as a camp director, the progressive Lieberman (1932, p. 10) was adamant that campers should be challenged to meet high standards and "be helped to greater achievement, but at their own pace and in activities that arise out of their own interests." He (p. 10) justified this position by maintaining that "if the activity represents the child's own purpose he will seek expert help so that he may gain skill and information and he will gain much strength from the process." This was an obvious shift towards a situation where more control was afforded to the camper.

Figure 10. Girls making lamp shades and weaving baskets in front of the Craft Hut, 1927 (photo courtesy of Camp Winnataska, Pell City, Alabama).

Bernard Mason (1930, p. 10) likewise stressed the importance of the "*present* interests of the campers," although he was also aware that the reaction against the highly regulated camp program may have swung too far at some camps and "developed into an opposite theory that the camp should be entirely free from schedule so far as activities were concerned." To some this shift towards the interests of the camper seemed to license a veritable free for all, reducing the role of counsellor to that of tag-along. But this was not what Lieberman (1932, p. 11) intended; his was not a "plea for a planless or chaotic camp":

> Such a course would bring about disastrous results. It is on the contrary a plea for a most thoroughly planned summer. The camp site must be chosen because it provides a stimulating and rich environment. The staff members must be chosen because of their capacity to stimulate interests and guide activity. Materials must be arranged so as to invite effort. The staff must be prepared to take advantage of the unexpected, to utilize spontaneous interests and occurrences, and utilize them in developing a larger plan. (Lieberman, 1932, p. 11)

Lieberman's program emphasized the importance of the child and method, in its relation to subject matter. His program was initially only minimally structured, thus requiring the campers to be intimately involved in the planning process. The central question was how involved the campers could be in the determination of the program. In their description of such a program, Dimock and Hendry's answer was a telling one, revealing the extent to which progressive camping had moved beyond traditional, adult-directed models:

> In camps of this type no program of an organized sort exists until it emerges from the needs and desires of the camp community. Subject matter or information is considered a part of the resources of the camp to be introduced to help meet a crisis, solve a problem, carry out a purposeful undertaking, or satisfy an interest in the present camp experience. Artificial incentives and controls consequently play an inconspicuous part. Campers and adults together share in the control and conduct of the camp society. (Dimock & Hendry, 1929, p. 42)

In her book chronicling the history of American summer camps, Leslie Paris (2008) reflects on Lieberman's insights into this situation. "Lieberman acknowledged that the progressive ideal was difficult to implement" (p. 243). There were "some camp leaders who kept abreast of the latest educational initiatives," and who "had tried to reshape their curricula to the latest trends," such as inclusion of "a free period each day for campers to choose an activity, new 'creative' activities like jewelry making, fewer awards, and greater use of educational terminologies" (pp. 243–244). However "they remained unsure how to replace competitive stimuli and adult-controlled programs" (p. 244). Thus, although "Lieberman concluded that progressive camp leaders' acknowledgement of children's individuality, however imperfectly realized, had changed the industry for the better" (p. 244), Paris echoed Lieberman's skepticism, pointing out that "the result of this experimentation … had been confusion." Again, even in camps – presumed to be uncontaminated by the strictures of schooling – the persistent societal confusion between subject matter (curriculum) and method (child) lurked below the surface.

DEVELOPING TIGHTER LINKS BETWEEN CAMPING AND SCHOOLING

The critical question of camping's relation to education raised the problem of the isolation of camp from everyday urban life. This isolation was a characteristic of a form of camping that had strongly appealed to those promoting its educational value, such as Bill Vinal, because it enabled a form of education that was, at face, radically different from school. Indeed, isolation had been touted as one of camping's fundamental virtues, especially from an educational perspective. "The camp is an environment isolated from organized society, and is thereby influenced by a minimum of direct supervision or control," camping legend L.B. Sharp (1930, p. 44) proclaimed. Because of this it presented "an ideal situation for the development of desirable attitudes and appreciations of freedom and democracy" (p. 44). However, its isolation – its main asset for some – was considered by others a serious limitation reducing the possibility for camp lessons to influence life more broadly.

> A qualifying statement should be made concerning the advantages of this "naturalness" of camp life which is so constantly stressed by camp directors and other writers. Camp life may be more "natural" than the city civilization if we are thinking of the biological and inherited psychological factors in the person. If the individual as social being is viewed realistically, however, the "civilized" life of the town or city is his natural habitat. Life in the woods is "unnatural." Wholesome values, satisfying activities and effective adjustments should characterize the normal community life of the individual. We may discover that the greater the hiatus between camp life and civilized life, the less the likelihood of transfer of the attitudes and habits stimulated in the camping environment. (Dimock & Hendry, 1929, p. 6)

While a believer in the educational possibilities of school camps, William Heard Kilpatrick (1929, p. xi) decried the fact that the camp was "intentionally removed from ordinary life" as an "abiding weakness in the camp." The camp "suffers from discontinuity: discontinuity in point of time – it runs only in the summer; discontinuity as regards life as a whole – it removes itself from people and it includes only one type of person" (p. xi). A significant downfall of such a situation was that "'transfer' of learning is lessened from what we should like" (p. xi). In spite of these limitations, however, Kilpatrick (p. xi) maintained that the summer camp stood "as a wonderful opportunity to show both school and home how education may be conducted on the inherent demands of education and life, two names for the same process if only we conceive them adequately." Kilpatrick (1942, p. 15) thus proffered that the camp "provides real living, and so brings learning far and away better than does the older type school. Hour for hour, a camp is often more educative than school because in it the children can better live what they learn."

Figure 11. L. B. Sharp (left, in hat) talking with Tom Rillo (right, in hat), another outdoor education pioneer, circa early 1950s at Sharp's National Camp – his leadership training camp for outdoor education in Pennsylvania (photo courtesy of Clifford Knapp).

In an attempt to overcome the inherent discontinuities of camp, proponents of progressive camping determined that camping "must be allied with other agencies in the community which are responsible for the development of the boy and girl" (Dimock & Hendry, 1929, p. 335). There was therefore a push for more connection with these other aspects of a child's life, founded in the belief that "the camping experience should be more closely related to the year-long experience of the camper" (p. 335). Hence, camping should be conceived as "an experience having all-year-round implications and as an education involving many educational and social agencies," Elmer Mitchell (1938, p. 142) declared. Obviously, a central aspect of the child's year round existence was school. So, by bringing camping within the gamut of the school the isolation of the camp would be reduced. Thus Mitchell voiced the belief that "the summer camping experience of the child is not an isolated one. It is tied up with all his other interests of the school year" (p. 142), a comment evidencing some awareness of what Dewey called continuity of experience. To this end the calls for a deliberately closer relation between camping and schooling grew louder. Herbert Twining (1938, p. 138) noted that while "camping and the activities of private schools have complemented one another for many years … it has only been during the past decade that serious consideration has been given to the possible relationship between the public school curricula and camping." Early in the 1930s, Ready (1933, p. 9) predicted that "within the next decade, many week end and day camping excursions will no doubt be included as a part of the regular school work carried on in public schools, and many summer sessions will be held entirely out of doors in camps," a prediction that turned out to be fairly accurate – at least for a time. Just over a decade later Rey Carlson (see figure 18) reported that "about sixty school systems in America are now experimenting with camping and outdoor education" (1947, p. 8).

Figure 12. L. B. Sharp tending his fire in his tipi at National Camp in Pennsylvania (photo courtesy of Clifford Knapp).

Of all the advocates for school camping, perhaps the most fervent was L.B. Sharp. He (1948, p. 315) believed it "educationally sound that school authorities should establish a school camp as an integral part of the total school plant," with the school camp seen as "a necessary facility just as much as the library, the gymnasium, the auditorium, and the laboratory." Sharp (1943, p. 367) anticipated a time "when every school" would "have its own campsite and operate it as an integral part of the total school program." And he (writing with E. G. Osborne) also held a more lofty hope regarding the impact of camps on schools:

> Is it possible to hope that teachers and administrators finding themselves a part of a more informal and free situation in summer camps will make strenuous efforts to bring something of the spirit, interest, and opportunity of this freer kind of environment into the school? How can the experiences of camps and schools become more unified? (Sharp & Osborne, 1940, p. 239)

For this dream to become a reality, Sharp realized that camping would need to be accepted as a genuine part of schooling. And for this to occur, those involved with camping had to gain legitimacy in addressing the school curriculum. Sharp (1943, p. 363) was adamant that "changes in the school curriculum would be made" and he coined the term *camping education* in order to describe the form of outdoor education he was promoting.

Camping education presents the basis for this change in the simple thesis: *that which ought and can best be taught inside the schoolrooms should there be taught, and that which can best be learned through experience dealing directly with native materials and life situations outside the classroom should there be learned.* Camping education is clearly an outdoor movement. This does not mean that it would all take the place of the school, but certainly it means that the school curriculum should be restudied and evaluated in terms of where is the best place to learn the things that are educationally worthwhile. A careful examination of subject matter and the curriculum on the basis of this simple thesis will unquestionably show that a far greater amount of the school time can more profitably be spent out-of-doors than is now the case with consequent gain to pupils. (Sharp, 1943, pp. 363–364)

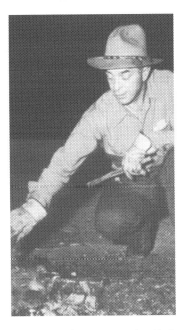

Figure 13. L. B. Sharp cooking a ritual evening meal at National Camp: a 'buffalo tro.'
A buffalo tro (slang for throw) meant cooking what was usually a beefsteak by throwing it directly on the coals (photo courtesy of Clifford Knapp).

Sharp (1947, p. 43) declared this minor manifesto as "the basic thesis of outdoor and camping education." So approximately four decades after its appearance, the banner of outdoor education was evolving to encompass school camping as a major part of its practice. Camping education, or school camping, would sit alongside the other educational programs considered part of an outdoor education. "It is certain," Julian Smith (1970, p. 4) later declared, "that organized camping had an important influence on the beginnings of outdoor education, coupled with the educational philosophies of Dewey, Kilpatrick, and others whose writings and leadership gave rise to 'progressive' education." The rise of camping education in the 1930s would precipitate a long and vibrant period in the middle 20th century whereby outdoor education was allied with general progressive aims. Thus, "the 1950s witnessed rapid development of school camping, and the term *outdoor education* began to be applied more generally" (Eells, 1986, p. 129).

Figure 14. Paddling together in the wilderness, 1948 (photo courtesy of Clearwater Camp for Girls, Minocqua, Wisconsin).

OUTDOOR EDUCATION AS METHOD AND SUBJECT-MATTER

Alongside Sharp's (1952, p. 20) principle of "using the out-of-doors wherever possible" came his understanding of educational method. "It has been proved in educational research that we *learn most through direct experience, we learn faster, the learnings are retained longer, and the appreciation is greater*" (1948, p. 314). The enormous breadth of subject matter content captured in the net of Sharp's thesis was unified through the method of outdoor education, a learning process that Sharp associated with *direct experience*.

> The evidence is clear that we learn best through direct experience. It has been proved that learning of this kind is faster, is retained longer, and is accompanied by deeper appreciation and understanding. Much, if not most, of the material in all subject matter areas at all levels that school youth study *about* in school can actually be *seen* and *experienced* firsthand outside the classroom and in the school camp. It is chiefly a problem of dividing this subject matter for inside and outside learning. (Sharp, 1947, p. 43)

Sharp enlisted Dewey to undergird his thesis and substantiate his claim about what could be learned through direct experience. He (1930, p. 37) cited Dewey's (1911, p. 400) definition of education, as listed in Monroe's *Cyclopedia of Education*, in his own early work: "Education may be defined as a process of the continuous reconstruction of experience with the purpose of widening and deepening its social content, while at the same time the individual gains control of the methods involved." However, where Dewey recognized the fundamental inseparability of content and process in human experience, and upbraided progressives for omitting subject matter from their theories (see Seaman & Rheingold, 2012; Westbrook, 1993), outdoor educators such as Sharp wittingly or unwittingly maintained their distinction. The tension between them would subsequently define outdoor education, as 'direct experience' became a core principle of the approach.

The tension inherent in Sharp's thesis was illustrated in a study conducted by Charles Lewis (1975) of much of the outdoor education literature published in the USA between 1948 and 1968. In his study, Lewis (p. 3) vigilantly compiled a list of seventeen hierarchically ordered "basic concepts of outdoor education" that were "formulated as the generally-accepted principles of outdoor education" contained in this published work. Each principle was based on "a minimum of three statements of evidence ... culled from the professional literature." The resulting list was then "presented to qualified practitioners and educators for validation" (p. 3). His aim was to then offer this list "for the consideration of those who desire to implement the method" (p. 3).

Figure 15. L. B. Sharp briefing a group of teachers at National Camp where they are to live for their period of residency during the leadership training program (photo courtesy of Clifford Knapp).

Coursing through Lewis's seventeen basic concepts was the tension between method and subject matter. His study revealed that those teaching and writing about mid-20th century outdoor education generally held the position that method was more important than subject-matter. As his (1975, p. 3) first basic concept stressed, "outdoor education is a *method* of education. It includes the use of the out-of-doors for the study of all areas of the curriculum when the subject matter can best be learned out-of-doors." One of the main sources Lewis used in the construction of this concept was Sharp's thesis. Sharp (1947, p. 43) did not suggest the learning of just any subject matter outdoors but only that subject matter which could "*best be learned*" there, leaving the determination of the appropriate subject matter to those involved in its teaching. In his second basic concept Lewis was more prescriptive about method and he also acknowledged some of the specific approaches encompassed under the banner of outdoor education. "The outdoor education method encourages the use of the environment outside the classroom and includes such experiences as field trips, excursions, vocational agriculture, and a school camp" (Lewis, 1975, p. 3). His third basic concept made the focus on method unequivocal: "outdoor education is not a separate discipline or a separate area of study such as history, English, arithmetic, or other subject matter areas" (p. 5). It was, in other words, decisively a method.

Figure 16. Camp Lincoln hikers climb Noonmark mountain in the Adirondacks, 1950s (photo courtesy of North Country Camps, Keeseville, New York).

Evident in Sharp's thesis, and in the basic concepts derived by Lewis, was an implicit claim that method should prevail whenever any conflict between method and subject matter should arise. Outdoor education was especially committed to using "*direct experience*" (Sharp, 1947, p. 43) to address a range of subject matter areas. Lewis's (1975, p. 5) fourth basic concept was the most emphatic in this regard. He echoed Sharp in stating that outdoor education was "designed to provide direct rather than vicarious experiences for students on the basis that the efficiency of education is increased in direct proportion to that direct experience." Central to Sharp's thesis was the distinction between learning through direct experience out-of-doors and learning about something vicariously indoors, in a classroom, often in ways that reduced the richness of direct experience to a more abstract symbolic representation. This emphasis can be clearly seen in what Lewis called his "summary concept statement" (p. 9), in which he encapsulated all seventeen of his basic concepts.

> Outdoor education is a direct, simple method of learning that extends the curriculum to the out-of-doors for the purpose of learning. It is based on the discovery approach to learning and it appeals to the use of the senses – audio, visual, taste, touch, and smell – for observation and perception. (Lewis, 1975, p. 9)

Based on his research, Lewis concluded that outdoor education was method first and subject matter second. To this end he did recognize certain content areas in some of his seventeen basic concepts. In concept seven, for instance, outdoor education was understood to enhance "the goals of conservation by enabling students to develop reverence for life through an ecological exploration of the interdependence of living things and assist them in developing a land ethic which illustrates man's[5] temporary stewardship of the land" (1975, p. 5). The eighth concept identified the "major emphasis" of outdoor education to be "the teaching of attitudes, appreciation, understanding, and expression rather than the mastery of techniques and bodies of factual information" (p. 6). And in concept nine outdoor education was acknowledged as providing "the opportunity to acquire basic skills, attitudes, and appreciation for leisure-time pursuits" (p. 6). While these concepts did not promote outdoor education as a body of knowledge as such, they did identify certain contextual understandings children were presumed to glean through the method of outdoor education – direct experience in the outdoors. Visible are two main categories around which these content areas cohere: the natural environment and outdoor leisure skills.

BEING OUT-OF-DOORS AND THE OUTDOORS

Although not directly referenced by Lewis, one conspicuous definition of outdoor education during this period endeavoured to explicitly encompass both method and subject matter. George and Louise Donaldson (1958) were, like Lewis, attempting to deal with the issue of defining outdoor education so as to better inform teachers and others who shared an interest in the approach. In addition, they perceived the need to try to reduce the confusion surrounding the term: "Words, especially definitive words, sometimes confuse a simple concept," they (p. 17) believed. In their estimation, "outdoor education is simple. It is as simple as a leisurely walk around the school grounds by a kindergarten teacher and her children." In order to capture this idea as elegantly and straightforwardly as possible, the Donaldsons (p. 17) famously rendered outdoor education as "education *in, about* and *for* the outdoors." But this attempt to forge a simple definition for outdoor education glossed over the significant tensions between the many different understandings of outdoor education that had preceded them, such as those evidenced in Lewis's seventeen basic concepts. So rather than achieving simplicity, the Donaldsons actually introduced further complexity and entrenched the confusion by creating three new divisions – *in, about* and *for* – with the relations amongst these three remaining open to question.

The Donaldsons acknowledged both method (*in* the outdoors) and subject matter (*about* the outdoors) in their definition. Both of these aspects of outdoor education worked together in their assessment that a method of direct experience *in* the out-of-doors could be applied in any area of the curriculum which was *about* the natural environment. In this way, while restating the accepted notion that outdoor education was a method applicable across the curriculum, the Donaldsons' definition more clearly emphasized the binary character of the term 'outdoors.' This term had been customarily employed in contrast to the notion of indoors, thereby expressing a move *out-of-doors* and away from the classroom. This was particularly evident in L.B. Sharp's work when he deliberately referred to outdoor education as out-of-door education. The Donaldsons' definition, however, emphasized the growing use of the term outdoors in reference literally to *the outdoors* – understood as the natural environment. In an educational sense, then, the Donaldsons precipitated the inevitable shift away from a focus on method concerned with being *out-of-doors* to one oriented towards subject-matter concerned with *the outdoors* as natural environment. This was, of course, not a new development but another of the various turns involving process and content that had dogged nature-study before outdoor education. The more open acknowledgement that specific academic content could be featured in outdoor education added to the tension between method and subject matter that inevitably surfaced in any sustained discussion of outdoor education. The Donaldsons had produced a seemingly simple definition that encompassed the breadth of outdoor education but in doing so had created a composite that did not address the underlying tension.

In a further play on the complexity inherent in the meaning of *outdoors*, the Donaldsons highlighted education *for* the outdoors. They (1958, p. 17) claimed that '*for* the outdoors' contained "the key word" of their definition: "*For* implies both a mental attitude toward the outdoors and a set of skills and abilities which will enable the learner to do something about his attitudes. Skills are not enough; neither are good attitudes without implementation" (p. 17). The Donaldsons thus married conservation attitudes towards *the outdoors* as natural environment, with outdoor recreation skills intended as leisure pursuits undertaken *in the out-of-doors. For* was meant to be the connecting factor, linking the out-of-doors and the outdoors (see figure 3).

These two senses of outdoor, as outdoors (the natural environment) and out-of-doors (a setting for recreation), mirrored the distinction Dewey (1916a, p. 196) highlighted between "*what* we experience (the experienc*ed*) and the experienc*ing* – the *how*," with the educational ramifications being that "when we give names to this distinction we have subject matter and method as our terms." The natural environment as experienc*ed* could be codified into subject-matter, while the out-of-doors as experienc*ing* referred to various methods for being out-of-doors. The Donaldsons laudably attempted to frame outdoor education as concerned at once with attitudes and knowledge, however, in handling each separately, their definition remained beholden to the emphasis on method or subject-matter and did not reconcile them as part of unified experience.

An earlier version of the Donaldsons' notion of *for* the outdoors was claimed by the Outdoor Education Project of the American Association for Health, Physical Education and Recreation (Smith, Carlson, Donaldson & Masters, 1972, p. 22) that began in 1955 and with which the Donaldsons were associated. Smith et al. (p. 22) described education *for* the outdoors as focused on the "skills, attitudes and appreciations necessary for intelligent use of the outdoors." These were skills "necessary for outdoor pursuits" that, while "often considered a part of physical education and recreation programs," also had "significance in science, conservation, health, safety, citizenship, and other subjects which cut across all curriculum areas" (p. 22). In tandem with this came "the development of attitudes concerning conservation" that were "an important part of learning outdoor sports such as camping, casting and angling, shooting, and hunting" (p. 22).

We note here for the reader, making a quick digression, that this sense of *for* has ramifications beyond method and subject matter in connection with Dewey's important notion of 'occupation,' which offers a way forward and out of this confusion. In other words, *for* highlights differing occupations which provide the meaningful framework within which certain methods and subject matters make sense. In this paragraph in Smith et al. (1972, p. 22), we can see different occupations being alluded to. We deal with Dewey's notion of occupation in much more detail in chapter six.

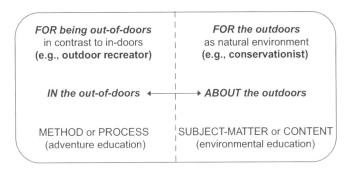

Figure 17. The differing emphases on method and subject-matter in each of outdoor education 'in' and 'about,' with 'for' the outdoors being applicable in different ways to both. Shown in brackets are alignments with adventure education and environmental education (to be covered in chapter 4), and the possible occupations associated with each understanding of 'for' (to be discussed further in chapter 6).

For Smith et al. (1972, p. 20), however, there was no sense that outdoor education could be constrained by the notion of *about* the outdoors, as outdoor education meant "learning *in* and *for* the outdoors." This was the position Smith (1960, p. 156) had articulated more than a decade earlier. The conscious omission of a specifiable area of content seemed especially important given the proclamation that "outdoor education is not regarded as a specialized or circumscribed area of learning" (Smith et al., 1972, p. 20). Thus Smith commented, "to circumscribe outdoor education – to separate its many teachable moments from the learning areas which characterize its diversity would render this new and fresh approach to learning less effective and would place it in the category of other 'special' kinds of education" (1970, p. 7).

Figure 18. Rey Carlson, Director of Bradford Woods Outdoor Centre at Indiana University, addressing a group during an outdoor education class in 1965 (photo courtesy of Clifford Knapp).

Equipped with this view, Smith campaigned strongly for an interdisciplinary understanding of outdoor education from his position as Director of the Outdoor Education Project at the American Association for Health, Physical Education and Recreation. He (1966, p. 3) described "the educational decade in which the Project emerged" as "characterized by contrasts." "On the one hand there were strong forces in support of the highly academic aspects of education. Gains made in outdoor education against this backdrop are remarkable," he (p. 3) commented, revealing the consistency of his belief in outdoor education as method, as education *in* the out-of-doors rather than *about* the outdoors. Pushing against these academic forces were others more favourable to education in the out-of-doors. "The climate for the emphasis on outdoor education has been good," Smith (p. 3) claimed, "particularly in view of the great surge of public interest in all forms of outdoor pursuits and in the current national developments in support of resources and programs." Here was outdoor education *for* being out-of-doors. From Smith's perspective, there was no need to emphasize any particular realm of subject matter, as this would simply constrain the important practical contribution outdoor education was making as method. Such academic constraint would simply limit outdoor education to a specific area of subject matter, rendering it as one amongst other school subjects rather than a method applicable to all.

Figure 19. Julian Smith (on the left of picture) receiving the first Taft Campus Outdoor Education award in 1970 from Don Hammerman, Director of the Lorado Taft Field Campus of Northern Illinois University (photo courtesy of Clifford Knapp).

Smith (1966, p. 3) described the efforts of "the Project" as progressing "on two fronts: interpreting the value of outdoor education in the learning process and in academic achievement; and in helping educate for a more 'literate' outdoor public." Here again we can see education *in* and *for* the out-of-doors. However Smith's advocacy on these two fronts exposed further ambivalence, especially amongst those in schools, where the existence of these two understandings of outdoor education simply exacerbated the longstanding confusion that was always just below the surface. Education *in* the out-of-doors and education *for* the out-of-doors were considered by some to be two different forms of education. One was about a method applicable across all school subjects (*in* the out-of-doors); the other was a form of education that seemed to focus on certain outdoor pursuits (*for* the out-of-doors). Hence the persistent question for those involved with school curricula was, as Blackman (1969, p. 5) expressed it: "How does outdoor education *fit* within the school program?"

The more I've focused upon using the out-of-doors for learning – education "in" the out-of-doors, the more I've become concerned that education "for" the out-of-doors may too easily become seen, in the eye of the non-outdoor educator, as being all of outdoor education. Thus, I'm left with the dilemma of how we can place primary emphasis upon utilizing the outdoor environment to enhance a wide range of learnings, yet not lose sight of the significant skills and understandings which better permit us to live in and utilize the outdoors as human beings – those things classified as "for" the outdoors. (Blackman, 1969, p. 5)

Education *in, about* and *for* the outdoors, while simple on one level, opened up many distinctions that resulted in a complex mix of differing versions of outdoor education. The need for a solution to this dilemma was urged particularly by those whose quest it was "to solidify a place for outdoor education in the curriculum" so that outdoor education could "become an integral part of the curricula of the American school" (Knapp, 1967, p. 8). With this goal in mind, Cliff Knapp (p. 8) provocatively claimed that "the greatest single weakness has been the development of a broad concept of the term [outdoor education]." "An all inclusive definition tends to render the term ineffective" (p. 8). He (p. 8) argued instead that "the term outdoor education should assume a meaning within the framework of modern educational structure." "Schools are placing more emphasis on academic programs," he (p. 12) noted. So, arguing against an exclusive commitment to method, Knapp proclaimed that "outdoor educators must rise to this challenge and support this need. Outdoor education cannot attempt a reversal of this trend, but must function within this structure if success is to be realized" (p. 12).

Figure 20. Cliff Knapp, with pencil on ear, teaching elementary education majors about contours, during an outdoor education class at Carbondale, Southern Illinois University in 1964 (photo courtesy of Clifford Knapp).

Knapp's (1967, p. 12) advice was for educators to choose between two viewpoints: one "outdoor recreation, camping," the other "phases of school and college curriculum." He also asserted his preference for which of these two emphases should prevail as outdoor *education*: "The meaning of the term should be reserved for use by educators in reference to outdoor curriculum" (p. 12). Outdoor education would not then encompass "the fields of camping and outdoor recreation," which Knapp (p. 12) believed "should remain as distinct professions." Instead, outdoor education was the outdoor curriculum, which altered "the regular indoor curriculum by increasing content and providing an effective means for learning the content" (p. 9). This refinement of the meaning of outdoor education was noted by Donaldson (1972, p. 9), who claimed that "the early 'holistic' approach" in outdoor education, "especially in resident programs, has been largely replaced by great emphasis on the academic." Mid-20th century outdoor education was going through the same reform cycle as its predecessor, nature-study, moving from a commitment to outdoor education as *method* to outdoor education as *subject matter.*

SUMMARY

In this chapter, we have outlined the cycles of reform that first appeared with nature-study in the late 1800s and continued through the progressive camping education movement in the mid 20th century. These waves of reform shared common phases. First, there was dissatisfaction with the traditional classroom-based system of education, combined with a concern for loss of firsthand contact with nature (and thus, from the perspective of cultural values, a loss of care for nature). Both of these were also usually married with a commitment to child-centeredness. Second, there appeared an ultimate shift toward and embrace of academic content as a crucial part of education – i.e., the outdoors specifically as, or at least allied with, subject matter. The pattern we have outlined thus began with commitments to method and eventually gave way to subject matter, laying the groundwork for yet another cycle.

Following on the heels of camping education in the 1960s, the confusion evident throughout the first half of the 20th century would be exacerbated with the emergence of another new movement: adventure-based outdoor education. While this new movement ushered in exciting new practices that leveraged popular outdoor activities, it did little to reconcile the method/subject matter dichotomy principally because it amplified the emphasis on direct experience without specification of subject matter. And, in some ways, adventure-based outdoor education actually sent the tension deeper underground by merging with constructivist and 'human potential' ideologies to treat method *as* subject matter. But, as we will show (with Dewey's help), even the explicit attempts during this period at refining the definition of outdoor education did little to offer a way out of the confusion between method and subject matter – a confusion that still confounds attempts at substantive educational reform involving the outdoors.

NOTES

[1]   While the term itself was not in general use before the 1880s, we shall continue to use the term nature-study with hyphen inserted following the example of Meyers (1910, 1911).

[2]   This training in zoology and botany was not of the university type we are familiar with today, but rather some coverage of these areas in a basic form gained by these individuals either in secondary (high) school or through normal school training.

[3]   Pyle (2001, p. 19) noted that "in 1911 Comstock published a large book called the *Handbook of Nature-Study*, replete with hundreds of lessons as well as relevant poems, photographs, and vignettes." Comstock's book enjoyed more success than Jackman's, and it "became one of the most universal texts in the American classroom" (p. 19).

[4]   Kliebard (2004, p. 137) notes that Kilpatrick was "an avowed disciple of Dewey's."

[5]   The use of man as a collective term is problematically dated but we have included it when used by other authors in quotations because of the difficulty posed by making changes. However we interpret this term as inclusive of all human beings and we do not employ it ourselves.

THE ENVIRONMENTAL CRISIS AND A DESIRE FOR ADVENTURE

OUTDOOR EDUCATION AND THE NATURAL ENVIRONMENT

The ongoing conflicts about outdoor education, characterized by differing viewpoints on whether outdoor education was *in*, *about* or *for* the outdoors – or some combination – was further influenced by a significant change in the way the natural environment was being considered in the USA and around the world. In the 1950s and 1960s "public concern for the environment has increased," McEvoy (1972, p. 221) reported, a judgment he based on a range of indicators including "a striking increase in the number of environmentally oriented articles appearing in US periodicals" (p. 218) and "a recent and sharp membership increase in the voluntary organizations which are most active in implementing preservationist environmental policies" (p. 220). McEvoy, an environmental sociologist, hypothesized two trends responsible for this change: "The first of these is the probable increase in Americans' personal exposure to their natural environments [chiefly by way of recreational activities]. The second is the clear and demonstrable deterioration in quality of many aspects of the natural rural and especially urban, environment" (p. 221).

Laszlo (1972, p. 14) connected this increase in public concern with the emergence of "a new concept of the environment," one which was "more reminiscent of classical Hellenic and Oriental modes of thought than of the technology adoring ethic of changing the world and improving it for human benefit." General conceptions of the character of the relation between people and nature were, ostensibly, becoming less dualistic and more integrated. "Man was long considered above or outside of nature – first as spectator, then a manipulator of it. In the new concept of the environment man is placed within nature, as an integral part of it" (p. 17). Such an understanding of the unity inherent to the relationship between human beings and nature had already been articulated within outdoor education and, of course, in indigenous communities for centuries (Roberts, 2012), but it was catching hold in educators' imaginations. As Bud Wiener (1967, p. 699) pointed out, "perhaps most basic to continued development [in outdoor education] is the recognition of ... the belief in the unity of nature and man's place in that unity."

> The outdoors as a setting for education, especially in more natural areas, exemplifies a uniqueness that abounds in beauty, mystery and power. Man as a part of a universal unity is challenged to discover, analyze, interpret and use that which surrounds him. (Wiener, 1967, p. 699)

Recognition of this unity, combined with the changes in public concern for the environment, underpinned a discernible shift in perception of the educational opportunities afforded by outdoor education. Just as outdoor education had initially offered an alternative to indoor education, it now came to be viewed as a bulwark against an impending environmental crisis. "This interest in natural areas and natural resource management during the Kennedy years caused many educators to examine and explore the school curriculum" (Kirk, 1975, p. 4). This was done with the aim of finding a way "to provide young Americans with a better understanding of their responsibility to use more wisely and, where possible, to replenish resources which were being consumed" (p. 4). Kirk (p. 4) maintained that, "of the entire educational fraternity, the segment best equipped to provide meaningful experiences which would develop an appreciation for land management were those of us engaged in outdoor education." Problematically however, when this environmental problem was merged with the other major factor that had shaped outdoor education's evolution – to counteract classroom based education – confusion was exacerbated, not reduced.

With the increasing characterization of the environment as a problem, considerations of outdoor education as *in*, *about* and *for* the outdoors became more strongly associated with the needs of the natural environment *per se*, causing educators to turn toward the emerging field of environmental education. In other words, *the environment* was eclipsing other possible meanings of *outdoor*. Lucas (1979, p. 50)[1] argued that "the label 'environmental education' makes literal sense when applied to a number of different classes of educative programs. It can refer to education *about* the environment, *for* the (preservation of the) environment or *in* the environment." For Lucas, both education *about* and *for* were specifically concerned with the environment.

> The programmes of education *for* the environment aim to assist the preservation or improvement of the environment for a particular purpose; contrast this with education *about* the environment, where the goal is a knowledgeable individual. Typical programmes *for* the environment will attempt to inculcate attitudes of concern for the features of the environment that enhance the chances of continued human life, which enhance the quality of man's life or which are claimed to have value in and of themselves. (Lucas, 1979, p. 52)

From Lucas's perspective, the only mode of environmental education that could be connected with education out-of-doors was education *in* the environment. "Education *in* the environment is characterized by the use of a particular pedagogic technique, whereas education *about* and education *for* the environment are characterized by the type of goals the programmes have" (Lucas, 1979, p. 54, emphasis in original). He further noted, alluding to the out-of-doors, that "the most general use of 'environment'" in the sense of *in* the environment was "the world outside the classroom" (p. 54).

OUTDOOR EDUCATION AND ENVIRONMENTAL EDUCATION

The method/subject matter confusion within outdoor education was now compounded by the conflation of outdoor education with environmental education. This tension was taken up directly by Phyllis Ford (1981, p. 1) who advanced the phrase "*Outdoor/ Environmental Education*," although she mainly used the term outdoor education. Ford (p. 12) selected the Donaldsons' definition (1958) as the basis for her own "recommended definition" of outdoor education, which even she called "overly simplistic." In contrast to the Donaldsons and Smith, Ford began with the premise that outdoor education was a subject in its own right, thereby taking outdoor education a further step towards a defined body of content knowledge. "It is this author's contention," she (1981, p. 69) proclaimed, "that outdoor education *is* a subject." Ford saw the choice as one between education and recreation. Like Knapp (1967), but with a slightly different emphasis, Ford (1981, p. 69) asked: "Is outdoor education the domain of educational agencies, or is it the domain of recreational agencies?"

> To many people in the United States, Canada, England, and Australia, outdoor education is synonymous with education for outdoor pursuits or recreational skills. Snowshoeing, cross-country skiing, winter survival skills, backpacking, fishing, hunting, and related outdoor pursuits that are physical in nature (i.e. nonmechanized) and rely on the natural environment for implementation are the sole topics .... On the other hand, as many or more people feel that outdoor education is outdoor science education and consists only of teaching about natural resources and their interrelationship. Between the two poles of this spectrum are many people who seem to compromise on some, albeit weak, combination of the two issues. There are also those who would not agree with either point of view, because they feel that outdoor education is not a separate subject, but rather a process of teaching (any subject) in the outdoors. (Ford, 1981, p. 69)

Ford's (1981, p. 12) interpretation of education *in* the outdoors as establishing "the location" of what she described as an "educational process" closely paralleled that of the Donaldsons (1958), Knapp (1967), Smith et al. (1972), and Lucas (1979). But for Ford, its method of 'direct experience' was not the defining aspect of outdoor education. Ford detailed a teaching progression that emphasized "problem-solving processes" (1981, p. 91) as a central feature. Yet these problem-solving processes would only be introduced following the acquisition *indoors* of academic content concerning ecology and environmental science. Only "after gaining an understanding of what occurs in every ecosystem" was the learner "prepared for and ready for outdoor education activities that teach the application of knowledge of the environment to the solution of problems related to it," she (p. 91) stipulated. And "the most commonly used problem-solving activities relate to soil, water, trees, and animals" (p. 91). This was, for Ford, unequivocally the subject matter of outdoor education.

Figure 21. Phyllis Ford speaking with Bud Wiener (photo courtesy of Clifford Knapp).

Ford (1981, p. 12) was aware that "education *about* the outdoors dictates subject matter and has thus produced controversy." "On this topic, outdoor educators are divided," she (p. 12) acknowledged. "Some believe that outdoor education *must* be about outdoor resources and/or outdoor skills, whereas others feel that outdoor education is not a subject, but a *location* and a *process* whereby one can learn any subject through the outdoors" (p. 12). Here Ford drew a distinction between education *about* the outdoors as subject-matter and interdisciplinary education *in* the outdoors. Ford's stance on outdoor education as a subject clarified her position in this controversy. She adopted a standpoint similar to Lucas (1979), who saw education *about* and *for* the environment as characterized by content-based curricular goals, while education *in* the environment was distinct from both, characterized as a pedagogic technique applicable in any subject. She advocated strongly for the former, her understanding of education *for* the outdoors closely aligning with outdoor education as subject-matter. Education *for* the outdoors was "for *use* of the outdoors: wise use for leisure pursuits; wise use for economic purposes" (1981, p. 13). It was also "for *understanding* the outdoors: understanding the relationship of natural resources to world survival; understanding the importance of a sense of stewardship; understanding our historical and cultural heritage (as read in the outdoors); understanding the aesthetics of the outdoors" (p. 13). Here both 'use' (as *wise* use) and 'understanding' were primarily considered not as method, but as the subject matter of outdoor education, as content to be taught.

ADVENTURE EDUCATION AND ENVIRONMENTAL EDUCATION

Adventure educator Simon Priest (1986) weighed into this "confusion associated with the definition of the term outdoor education" (p. 15) with the aim of "redefining outdoor education" (p. 13). Like Ford, Priest (p. 13) highlighted the Donaldsons' definition, calling it "the classic definition of outdoor education." Yet at the same time he noted that this definition had been "criticized from many viewpoints" (p. 13). Priest therefore abandoned the attempt to simply discuss what else outdoor education was *in*, *about* and *for* and instead strove to develop a new framework that encompassed both being out-of-doors and the outdoors itself. He took issue with the dichotomy others seemed to promulgate, especially the emphasis on the natural environment which grew from the environmental movement. His approach was to broaden the definition by re-incorporating the dormant out-of-doors element. "Some believe that the purpose of outdoor education is not sensible stewardship, but independent learning, free thinking, and self-reliant problem solving," Priest (p. 13) claimed. "Others feel that there is more to learn about than just the outdoor environment" (p. 13). These others "claim that the personal environment and socialization are equally important topics which lend themselves to outdoor education learning situations" (p. 13).

Capturing these differing perspectives, Priest (1986, p. 14) identified two main forms of outdoor education: "environmental education" and "adventure education." He maintained that outdoor education should be the banner or umbrella encompassing both of these forms. This put him at odds with Ford, Lucas, and others who believed that the proper banner was environmental education. "An expansion of outdoor education is environmental education, which is broader and all inclusive," Ford (1981, p. 14) remarked. Kirk (1975, p. 15) also considered environmental education to be more fundamental, as well as urgent, created when "environmental problems increased in significance and number" thereby forcing "the philosophical components of outdoor education and conservation education[2] on a collision course." As the external pressures of the environmental crisis increased, Kirk (p. 15) considered a blending of outdoor education and conservation education to have occurred, resulting in a "quantum jump which produced the field of environmental education."

Proponents of the phrase environmental education, however, virtually ignored adventure education, which was rising in popularity. Adventure education appeared to merge camping and outdoor recreation and highlighted the personal and social aspects of being out-of-doors away from traditional modes of education. Its early expansion in the 1960s was attributable to three main cultural and educational trends. First was "the emergence of widespread interest in such outdoor sports as backpacking, mountaineering, cross-country skiing, and bicycle touring, between 1965 and 1974" (Wilson, 1977, p. 54). These outdoor pursuits began to rival fishing and hunting as the primary ways to educate *for* being out-of-doors. Referring to a study of the "comments and writings of the new wilderness sport participants," Wilson (p. 55) revealed that "their involvement was motivated by two closely related desires. One quite simply was the wish to escape the technology and urbanization of modern living. The second was the desire to achieve a greater sense of self-awareness."

*Figure 22. Kurt Hahn addressing an audience at The Athenian School in northern
California in 1965 (photo courtesy of The Athenian School archive).*

Second amongst these cultural and educational trends was the importation of German educator Kurt Hahn's ideas into elite boarding schools along with the adaptation of his UK-based Outward Bound program to a US context (Miner & Bolt, 1981). A closely related third influence was the widespread growth of a humanistic, self-help ethos in the 1970s, which ushered in new forms of interpersonal training, including in the very schools where adventure was taking root (Armstrong, 1990). Outdoor education thus came to be seen as a prime vehicle for personal development (Katz & Kolb, 1968; Vokey, 1987), and as adventurous sports became incorporated into education programs, the focus on self improvement through outdoor pursuits became central: "the defining characteristic of adventure *education* is that a conscious and overt goal of adventure is to expand the self, to learn and grow and progress toward the realization of human potential" (Miles & Priest, 1990, p. 1).

> While adventure education programs may teach such skills as canoeing, navigation, rock climbing and rappelling, the teaching of such skills is not the primary goal of the enterprise. The learnings about the self and the world that come from engagement in such activities are the primary goals. (Miles & Priest, 1990, p. 1)

Hahn's (1957) Outward Bound program, first developed in the UK in the 1930s and 1940s, indelibly influenced adventure education in the US and many other countries: "any history of adventure education must start with Hahn," announced Miles and Priest (1990, p. 53). As Outward Bound arrived in the United States in 1962 (Zook, 1986, p. 55), Hahn's wartime emphasis on "muscular Christianity" gave way to a new focus on self-improvement and social relations (Freeman, 2011; Millikan,

2006). In their account of the first Outward Bound course to run in the USA, for instance, Miner and Bolt (1981, p. 103) commented on "the ultimate discovery" by each participant "that more than anything else Outward Bound is a revelation of people's interdependence and a challenge to their ability to work together."

Figure 23. Students and instructors at Hurricane Island Outward Bound School prepare for a round-the-island overnight hike with homemade backpacks – another test of their individual initiative and craftsmanship – at Cross Island in 1967 (photo courtesy of Jim Garrett).

In this tradition, learning about the environment was secondary to using the environment to learn about the self and others. But such a seemingly definitive understanding of outdoor education as adventure education was still tempered by old divisions, as evidenced in the story of Outward Bound expatriate Paul Petzoldt, who helped establish "the first American Outward Bound program in Colorado and became chief instructor" (1974, p. 13). In 1965 Petzoldt moved on from Outward Bound to found the National Outdoor Leadership School, whose lengthy wilderness expeditions looked superficially like Outward Bound but where "perhaps" the "most important purpose" was "to teach practical conservation" (p. 14).

Predictably, debates ensued concerning distinctions between adventure education and environmental education. Yet for many, these two remained elements of a broader idea of outdoor education. Priest, for one, conceived of this larger whole as one built on different types of relation. From this perspective environmental education was concerned with the relational features within nature itself, as well as with human-nature relations. But these were not the only relations significant in outdoor education. There were also those relations important to adventure education, specifically psychological aspects of the self as well as social relations among those who pursued adventures, which in the case of Outward Bound occurred in the prescribed group size of 8–15 members (Walsh & Golins, 1976).

*Figure 24. Flanked by his. cooking gear – #10 cans, one of which has been
fashioned into a Hibachi stove – a student waves to signal that all is well during
his Solo experience during an Outward Bound course at Hurricane Island in
the 1960s (photo courtesy of Jim Garrett).*

Even though recognized as a foremost adventure educator, Priest ostensibly shared
with environmental educators their urgent, conservationist attitudes. "Adventure
approaches," he wrote, "need to deal with environmental issues if they are to
protect the setting they treasure so greatly .... And environmental approaches
need to develop confident individuals who solve problems cooperatively and
who can make sound judgments regarding the stewardship of our planet" (1986,
pp. 14–15). He considered the two primary relationships in adventure education
to be intrapersonal and interpersonal, while the two of greatest concern for
environmental education were ecosystemic and ekistic: "Adventure education
programs, involving outdoor pursuits, have traditionally concentrated on the
intrapersonal and interpersonal relationships" (p. 14). Alternatively "environmental
education programs, involving ecological studies, have traditionally concentrated
on the ecosystemic and ekistic relationships" (p. 14). However, as they undoubtedly
blended together in actual outdoor education practice, Priest sought an integrated
definition: "each approach may still retain a primary focus on one pair of
relationships but would also, by the very nature of being outdoors, touch on the
other two" (p. 14). Employing these understandings, Priest (p. 13) tried innovatively
to cut through the confusion by offering a "redefinition of the term outdoor
education":

> *Outdoor education is an experiential process of learning by doing, which takes
> place primarily through exposure to the out-of-doors. In outdoor education
> the emphasis for the subject of learning is placed on RELATIONSHIPS,
> relationships concerning people and natural resources.* (Priest, 1986, p. 13)

Importantly, Priest's emphasis on relationships was not achieved by focusing on common content but rather by placing the notion of direct experience first and foremost in considerations of outdoor education. Through 'learning by doing,' participants would discover the inherent connections between self, others, and nature. Unlike Ford, he did not emphasize academic content as primary to engagement with the outdoors; it was direct experience that enabled any content to be encountered, any relationship to be capitalized on for educational ends. "Through exposure to the outdoor setting individuals learn about their relationship with the natural environment, relationships between the various concepts of natural ecosystems, and personal relationships with others and their inner Self," Priest (1986, p. 15) argued.

Priest introduced holism to outdoor education at a time marked by division, but in retrospect a similar notion had been with outdoor education from its early days; historically this was not a new development. L.B. Sharp had already noted how the direct experience of camp determined the subject matter of camp. "Various problems arise out of the natural process of caring for one's self, adjusting to the environment, and enjoying activity in camp and particularly in the more primitive conditions of the small camping units, overnight camping, and outpost camps" (1930, p. 45). And it is "these problems" that "afford the primary opportunities for learning in camp life" (p. 45). Sharp (pp. 45–46) summed these problems up by describing them as "*matters of hygiene*," "*matters of a sense of civic responsibility – the essence of citizenship*," and "*matters of nature*"; or in other words, relationships among self, others and nature.

OUTDOOR EDUCATION AS EXPERIENTIAL EDUCATION

One can infer from Priest's definition that direct experience was to be given foremost consideration in outdoor education, especially adventure education. If an 'experience' was conducted properly, children could learn whatever subject matter was at hand, and probably even some that weren't explicitly intended. In other words, these discoveries were enabled by proper *methods*. Of course subject matter could not be disconnected from method; direct experience (experienc*ing*) was an experience of *something* (experienc*ed*). Notably, however, Priest's definition subtly reversed the priorities of environmental education, especially in the accounts of Ford and Lucas. There direct experience tended to take a back seat to subject matter, which framed the design of educational experiences. Subject matter came first, thereby necessitating a design geared towards learning pre-specified knowledge. An initial learning experience was usually indoor and classroom based, augmented with a fieldtrip that would help people establish firsthand knowledge of the content. Yet, among advocates of direct experience, even a fieldtrip of this type could be construed as insufficiently direct. It was, in essence, a continuation of indoor education, yielding data or other observations connected with a problem or issue already introduced in advance by the teacher. Having been encountered in this way, the problem was likely to remain owned by the teacher, rather than emanating from students' own firsthand activity. Direct experience thereby contained an implicit emphasis on method.

The period of experiential education. It was during a 1974 conference in the US oriented towards outdoor pursuits that the focus on direct experience as method secured its place in the pantheon of late 20th century reforms: "experiential education" became a new watchword that fuelled a movement (Garvey, 1990). The advocacy for experience as method was now not confined to adventure education but was taken up by others as well; subsequent conferences attracted not only those with an interest in Outward Bound-style programs but "regular classroom teachers" too, as Dan Garvey (p. 77) described them. It seemed to these early members of the Association for Experiential Education that "outdoors people were coming indoors and indoor people were moving outdoors" (Shore & Greenberg, 1978, p. 45). Direct experience became a central pillar of outdoor education.

We want to take a quick detour here and bring Dewey more directly into the conversation, as most discussions about the educative value of direct experience situate themselves in Deweyan territory. Experiential education is certainly no exception to this; he is recognized by many as one of "the forefathers of experiential education" (Breunig, 2011, p. 62). But what many reformers overlook is the fact that Dewey found advocacy-based arguments about 'direct experience' in education to be very problematic (a significant reason behind his equivocal support of reforms such as manual training and home credits). It was clear to him that even in the traditional classroom, where the focus was chiefly on subject matter, experiences were being had: "It is a great mistake to suppose, even tacitly, that the traditional schoolroom was not a place in which pupils had experiences" (1938, p. 26). Indoor classroom experiences had their own structure and meaning, often geared towards the learning of subject-matter for the purposes of testing and grading and the eventual, supposed mastery of a defined and logical body of knowledge. Dewey had a more complex stance on subject matter than its discovery in *direct experience*, arguing that it "must be restored to the experience from which it has been abstracted. It needs to be psychologized" (1902b, p. 22). In other words, despite the reality that classroom experiences were direct in their own special way, the meaning of subject-matter could not be disconnected from how it gained *initial* significance in non-classroom human activity. Notably, Dewey's position here differs from both Ford's, who wanted subject matter emphasized *prior to* a non-classroom experience, and Priest's, who emphasized direct experience generically as capable of addressing an array of subject matter goals. Dewey's argument on this point was not well developed by subsequent reformers, particularly experiential educators championing adventure-based activity in the outdoors. We will return to this point in Chapter 6.

Without consciously doing so, advocates of experiential education were recreating the same reform cycle that nature-study and camping education had undergone years before. For example, Richard Kraft (1985, p. 7) wrote that "the immediate reasons for the reanalysis of the role of experience in learning" came "from the failure of contemporary schooling to meet the needs of large portions of youth." Further to this, "every major national study of the problems of youth, adolescents and the secondary schools and universities in the 1970s made similar recommendations concerning the need for experiential modes of learning" (p. 7), a necessity prescribed "for most, if not all youth, in the last quarter of the twentieth century." Zajchowski (1978, p. 12) made a similar observation when he asserted that "experiential education is the keystone of current educational reform literature." The motivational problems with classroom-based education were again a central issue. The pedagogical response, however, now bore the name *experiential education*, a movement that highlighted the association between method and experience, a connection Sharp had earlier acknowledged. Hammerman (1980, p. 126) predicted that this next cycle of development in outdoor education "might well be labelled – 'The Period of Experiential Education.'"

The period of experiential education involved a more refined turn to method. Method was now the process of experiencing, placing major emphasis on manipulating the structures of experience itself. Efforts by those concerned with experiential education to model these structures drew inspiration from Dewey, with obvious significance being given to the connection between experience and education – the title of one of his books published in 1938. There Dewey characterized thinking as an active process of inquiry, a form of 'doing' in its own right (see also Dewey, 1933). In experiential education, however, a distinction was often drawn between doing and thinking; a dichotomy that was encoded in dominant conceptions of experiential learning adopted during this period. "Experience [doing] alone is insufficient to be called experiential education, and it is the reflection process which turns experience into experiential education," wrote experientialist Laura Joplin in 1981 (p. 17). Experiential education was constituted by "an 'action-reflection' cycle" (p. 17). So, while doing or action was important, learning depended on a subsequent moment of thinking – or 'reflection' as it came to be called. Joplin (p. 19) referred to this reflecting process as a "debrief." In their textbook for adventure educators, Simon Priest and Michael Gass (1997, pp. 144–146) identified a number of experiential education models that expressed this basic structure, including David Kolb's (1984) theory of experiential learning and development, as well as ideas drawn from Dewey. We discuss this conception in greater detail in the next chapter, presenting an alternative reading of Dewey.

The period of experiential education in outdoor education is most clearly marked by this emphasis on doing or activity followed by reflection. Notably, this design structure stems less from any affiliation with conservationist attitudes or environmental knowledge, but from its philosophical commitment to self-improvement and its pedagogical emphasis on direct experience as method. As Hammerman (1980, p. 126) acknowledged, this was "a period in which the 'form' or 'structure' of the program (e.g., residential)" was "not the most important factor to be considered, but one in which the learning processes and teaching strategies are of greater significance." Although prominent advocates of experiential education drew directly or indirectly on Dewey to advance their claims, the emphasis on the *process* of learning, rather than its *contents,* did little to alleviate the longstanding educational confusion between method and subject matter he tried repeatedly to overcome.

The debate, of course, continued to play out in the practical and scholarly literature. Ted Wichmann (1980), commenting on significant early developments in experiential learning theory, criticized the one-sided nature of this emphasis. "Walsh and Golins (1976), Gager (1977) and Greenberg (1978) have all developed process-centered experiential learning theories" (p. 9). However, while "each of these three papers describes in detail how the experiential learning process flows, ... all avoid any detailed discussion of *what* is to be learned" (p. 9). Wichmann called this "the process-centered syndrome." A year later, in their historical account of experiential education's evolution from progressivism, Albert Adams and Sherrod Reynolds (1981) described a similar realization:

> It is evident that [current experiential reforms] have retained what Ed Yeomans, an historian of the progressive movement, fondly refers to as the 'adventure, romance, and life in community' reminiscent of the early Romantics. But the corresponding emphasis on academic rigor and an integrated approach to the arts in many instances has been minimized or eliminated. (p. 27)

Priest's relational redefinition of outdoor education, discussed above, can be read as an attempt to address Wichmann's point and forge some connection, however loose, to subject matter. However, Priest's focus on relationships was in practice so broad an identification of content that it lent little specificity to outdoor education, which again was serving as a banner term covering an ever growing list of educational initiatives. Thus, in the 1980s and 1990s, with no substantial resolution to Dewey's 'confusion,' outdoor education was still contributing to the major problem of the crowded curriculum rather than offering any fundamental reform strategy for education.

A RECENT TURN: OUTDOOR EDUCATION AS PLACE-BASED EDUCATION

Although adventure education usually occurred in the outdoors, environmental knowledge or conservationist values were not emphasized or even necessary to the approach. Nature had, to some critics, become a mere backdrop for self-discovery rather than a focus in its own right; worse than mere anthropocentrism, this could be seen as a kind of narcissism. Any environmental understanding or commitment to conservation was purely incidental: as Seaman and Rheingold (2012) write, "the idea became that where learning occurs is less important than what you, personally, learn about yourself" (p. 260). One study even found a wilderness-based adventure program to be detrimental to students' attitudes toward and understanding of nature (Haluza-deLay, 2001). Some critics have gone further, suggesting that the preoccupation with self-improvement actually exploits nature for human gain, thereby promoting a self-absorbed kind of individualism that tacitly indoctrinates people to the divisive values of global capitalism rather than promoting any kind of ecological harmony (Bowers, 2005; Brookes, 2002).

Educators in the critical theory tradition have long made this argument about mass schooling in general (see Apple, Au & Gandin, 2009). Schools' emphasis on abstract, universal knowledge, they maintain, devalues and detracts from the practical, local concerns that people are most knowledgeable about, have most control over, and have the greatest stake in improving. Some environmental educators who share this perspective (see Orr, 2002) sought to give nature, especially in local places, a more prominent role in outdoor educational practice. Thus emerged *place-based education,* what Woodhouse and Knapp (2000, p. 2) called "a recent trend in the broad field of outdoor education." It is "a relatively new term, appearing only recently in the education literature" (p. 6). David Gruenewald (2003a, p. 3) connected place-based education with other reforms such as "… experiential learning, contextual learning, problem-based learning, constructivism, outdoor education, indigenous education, environmental and ecological education, bioregional education, democratic education, multicultural education, community-based education, critical pedagogy …, as well as other approaches," but especially those "concerned with learning from and nurturing specific places, communities, or regions." At the start of the 21st century, "place" became a preeminent concern in outdoor experiences.

According to Smith (2002, p. 586), the aim of place-based education "is to ground learning in local phenomena and students' lived experience." Yet Gruenewald argues that place-based education is an advance over old priorities, not simply education *in* the out-of-doors, a method for teaching that which could "*best be learned*" there, as Sharp (1943, p. 364) had put it. "In order to avoid the common assumption that place-based education is merely a methodology or technique through which to deliver standard school curriculum," Gruenewald (2005, p. 263) stresses "a philosophical orientation that embraces place as a construct fundamental to the purpose, process and structure of schooling."

Gregory Smith (2002, p. 594) contends that "the primary value of place-based education lies in the way it serves to strengthen children's connections to the regions in which they live." Important here are "local phenomena ranging from culture and politics to environmental concerns and the economy" (p. 594). For example, Gruenewald (2005, p. 263) emphasizes "place consciousness" and suggests "an awareness of *other* places beyond one's own local environment; fostering such an awareness and examining the interrelationship between places, such as the local Walmart and the distant factories that produce and export cheap goods." Here *place* is not only the outdoors taken as natural environment; it is a window into humankind's role in the social and natural ecology. As Smith (2007, p. 190) acknowledges, "place-based education can be distinguished from much conventional environmental education by the attention its practitioners direct toward both social and natural environments." Places, as social and natural environments, are settings beyond the classroom door that form an integrating context for a variety of subject-matter.

In Dewey's terms, place-based education could be considered the most recent version of the 'new education.' As such, it is likely in the early stages of the reform cycles Meyers (1910) identified and we have been describing as occurring throughout the 20th century. Gruenewald (2005, p. 274) made a similar point: "as a relatively recent phenomenon, place-based or place-conscious education has not yet subjected itself to the gaze of governmentality to the extent witnessed in current EE [environmental education] discourse." In other words, "place-based education … has not yet been widely institutionalised" (p. 263). Place-based educators might look to nature-study to consider the possibility of a future Gruenewald points to. With nature-study there had been "a recognition of the fact that children are instinctively interested in their nature environment; that their reactions to these interests exert on them a strong growth influence – physically, mentally, spiritually" (Meyers, 1910, p. 212). What followed from this recognition was the desire among curriculum experts "to utilize this interest" (p. 212). In the next stage of the cycle, knowledge might be "systematized" (p. 212), subject matter developed as an assessable body of knowledge that defines the study of place and places.

As Gruenewald (2003b, p. 621) possibly foretells, "where place-conscious traditions continue, they will be under constant pressure to prove their worth by conventional measures in national, state, and local systems of education."[3] Educators might further predict that an emerging emphasis on subject-matter may bring place-based education more and more indoors, where it will be subject to the trappings of traditional school. Then a new effort would emerge at some point, designed to fill the gap created by the institutionalization of place-based education, which would again aspire to reach the student-centered ideals of progressive education. Under these conditions, place-based education would itself not disappear but would become yet another contributor to the crowded curriculum.

SUMMARY

Throughout the 20th century, outdoor education as a pedagogical approach enjoyed periods of success as well as struggle. These periods followed a discernable pattern; just as the early nature-study had become botany and the so-called 'fads and frills' such as camping education were superadded to a fixed system of schooling, the various cycles of reform reproduced the underlying dualism of method and subject-matter, and what resulted was crowding in the curriculum rather than a fundamental re-imagining of education as a cultural institution. Outdoor education has thus refracted over a century into an increasing array of different hybrids. As stated in the introduction, such proliferation prompted Knapp (1997, p. 4) to compile "a list of more than 50 terms that fit under the umbrella describing our field."

> … earth education, ecological education, energy education, expeditionary learning, environmental and environment education, adventure and challenge

education, outdoor ethics education, bioregional education, science-technology-society education, global environmental change education, and sustainable development education. Just look in any professional conference program for some of these terms and for the variety of activities offered. (Knapp, 1997, p. 4)

Knapp's recognition of the crowded curriculum indicates the deeper issue we have been trying to illustrate. As Kraft (1985, p. 8) pointed out, "one of the major problems of the experiential education movement has been its inability to agree upon a definition. This makes the task of finding the philosophical, psychological and other underpinnings of the emerging discipline that much more difficult." Kraft (p. 8) identified what he believed was "perhaps the broadest possible definition" of experiential education in the writings of Morris Keeton, Executive Director of the Cooperative Assessment of Experiential Learning, who called it "that which 'occurs outside of classrooms' (Keeton, 1976, p. 5)." Astute readers will detect a restatement of outdoor education as it was originally pitted against classroom-based education nearly a century before. This recurrent history suggests the cycles of reform will continue, leading to ever more crowding in the curriculum rather than a fundamental transformation of what *outdoor education* might mean in the context of schooling.

NOTES

[1] This book, published in Australia, is a close adaptation of Lucas's (1972) PhD thesis gained at Ohio State University.

[2] Conservation education was a precursor to environmental education that "focused on assisting both youth and adults in understanding more fully the characteristics, distribution, status, uses, problems, and policies regarding natural resources" (Stapp, 1974, p. 46). It signals how a sense of 'for the environment' (conservation) could be understood as primarily concerned with subject matter.

[3] Jennings, Swidler and Koliba (2005, p. 62) queried "the relationship between standards-based reforms and place-based education" in Vermont, where two place-based standards were developed and incorporated into the already existing curriculum standards framework. Their research "suggested that the conflict between standards and place-based curriculum may be more rhetorical than real" (p. 63). They (p. 62) also pointed out that these place-based standards were "not embedded in the part of the frameworks – the fields of knowledge – that are currently being assessed," and this reduced the emphasis on specific content. But this situation was beginning to change. "Vermont policy makers are considering designing assessments for the Vital Results section of the frameworks," they (p. 62) acknowledged, right where the place-based standards were situated.

MOVING PAST THE CONFUSION: WHAT IS *EDUCATION*?

A PROBLEM OF EDUCATION, NOT JUST OUTDOOR EDUCATION

We began this book by asking 'What is outdoor education?' and have attempted to show how this seemingly trivial (although fraught) question points to a deep and abiding problem with institutionalized schooling, rather than suggesting a tidy new version of reforms that provide specific solutions to problems with 'indoor' education. Throughout the book we have invoked specific points from Dewey's work, and our discussion of solutions will turn to him more directly. We are also borrowing from Dewey in our *approach* to offering solutions; he understood that before one can propose solutions, some basic agreement is needed on the problem. For "to see the problem another sees, in the same perspective and at the same angle – that amounts to something. Agreement in solutions is in comparison perfunctory" (1906, p. 129). The recurrent debates about method and subject matter in outdoor education suggest that there is not yet common agreement on the problem – which, according to Dewey, really stems from evasion of the question: 'What is *education*?' While we'd like to think our last two chapters are more than 'perfunctory,' we keep our focus at a level deeper than specific prescriptions.

Up to now, we have argued that outdoor education's 'basic problem' is underlying confusion which manifests itself in ongoing debates about the centrality of method versus subject matter, a problem that is especially apparent once one recognizes cyclic patterns of reform over more than a century. Notably, this problem situates outdoor education within debates and discourses relevant to education more broadly. Chapters two to four outlined how competing priorities were advanced in the face of perceptions of the failure of schools to engage children on the one hand, and impart to them important academic content on the other hand. We described how outdoor education reforms have vacillated from one of these poles to the other and back again. We also highlighted some of the reformers who tried to deal explicitly with these issues – some arguing strongly for prioritizing method, others for subject matter, and still others trying to rise above the fray and resolve the conflicts between them. In spite of these efforts, deep conflicts have persisted, as outdoor education's relationship to schooling remains as fractured and tenuous as ever.

We hope we have convinced readers to perceive outdoor education's history as we do: first, as a series of important reform movements that addressed serious and evolving environmental, social, and psychological issues; and second, as emblematic of deeper issues in education that invariably result in its marginalization and/or joining an already crowded curriculum. For we believe it is important to understand that confusion is not characteristic of outdoor education alone, but rather is a longstanding feature of institutionalized education more generally. Until underlying confusion is addressed, such will be the plight of most reforms. As Dewey (1938) expressed, with some exasperation, in the final paragraph of his small but powerful book *Experience and Education*, the conflict between new and old education, progressive and traditional education, method and subject matter, child and curriculum, should not be accepted as somehow fundamental and basic. Instead educators must continue to pursue this problem to a deeper level, to finding out what education *is*.

> I have used frequently in what precedes the words "progressive" and "new" education. I do not wish to close, however, without recording my firm belief that the fundamental issue is not of new versus old education nor of progressive against traditional education but a question of what anything whatever must be to be worthy of the name *education*.... The basic question concerns the nature of education with no qualifying adjectives prefixed. What we want and need is education pure and simple, and we shall make surer and faster progress when we devote ourselves to finding out just what education is and what conditions have to be satisfied in order that education may be a reality and not a name or a slogan. (Dewey, 1938, pp. 90–91)

We are sympathetic to Dewey's appeal and also hope for an educational future that requires no 'qualifying adjectives' prefixed to education, even that of *outdoor*. To propose such a future, we will try and inhabit Dewey's imagination in the above passage when he argues that teachers and others have been fundamentally confused about what education *is*.

UNDERSTANDING EDUCATION AS EXPERIENCE

In the preface of *Experience and Education*, Dewey (1938, p. 5) argues that "it is the business of an intelligent theory of education to ascertain the causes for the conflicts that exist." (Like Dewey, we have proposed that many conflicts have their origins in dichotomous ways of thinking about method and subject matter, child and curriculum.) But "instead of taking one side or the other," this intelligent theory should "indicate a plan of operations proceeding from a level deeper and more inclusive than is represented by the practices and ideas of the contending parties" (p. 5). Going to this deeper level, however, does not mean attempting "to bring about a compromise between opposed schools of thought, to find a *via media*, nor yet make an eclectic combination of points picked out hither and yon from all schools" (p. 5). In other words, innovative solutions cannot be achieved merely by selecting the most attractive parts of competing theories; a new and comprehensive approach is required. Dewey attempted such an approach by using his vast concept of *experience*, to which we now turn. A note to readers: we will need to go afield of outdoor education for a time to lay some new groundwork in this area before we can situate it again as part of schooling.

In order to get beyond the compromises and hybrids that have characterized education reforms for a century, including outdoor education, it is necessary to understand how method and subject matter invariably work together in a unified way rather than simply considering them as separate and thus in conflict. To achieve this it will be instructive to return to Dewey's core idea "that there is an intimate and necessary relation between the processes of actual experience and education" (1938, p. 20). In other words, there is no need to make education 'more experiential'; in fact, this orientation reflects a misunderstanding of *experience* and is already off on the wrong foot. But how then, did Dewey want educationists to approach their field, equipped with a notion of *experience*?

We'll approach this question in three steps over the next two chapters. First, in this chapter, we discuss how Dewey broke down the thinking/doing dualism that underlies the subject matter/method dichotomy. We'll explain how Dewey's theory has been approached wrongly particularly by the most recent wave of outdoor education reforms, what Hammerman (1980) called the period of experiential education. We introduce an important aspect of Dewey's theory that has been largely overlooked, the relationship between *reflective* and *aesthetic* experience, and show how, even in *reflective experience,* Dewey argued against a doing/thinking dichotomy. Second, we'll discuss how Dewey situated his theory in recent human history, particularly as large-scale social institutions were established and specially designed to promote 'learning.' This historical overview is important to understanding how Dewey saw the fundamental relationship between doing and learning in experience and why he argued that reformers made critical errors that doomed both their child-centered and subject area projects. Finally, in the next chapter, we describe the educational program Dewey developed on the back of these ideas, in which *experience* and *education* were unified. A core part of Dewey's program is the concept of *occupations.* We conclude the book by imagining outdoor education not as a method or a subject area, but as a series of occupations that would indispensably shape any education that could be considered worthwhile. Such occupations meaningfully *incorporate* method and subject matter, providing that deeper level which gets beneath the problem and opens up an area of discourse in outdoor education and education more generally that is easily overlooked.

Reflecting on 'reflection.' The predominant way of organizing outdoor education during its most recent period has been to emphasize connections between *experience* and *reflection.* This emphasis is often attributed to Dewey, apparently stemming from a reading of his short book *Experience and Education* (Miettinen, 2000). For example, one popular adventure education textbook refers to it when claiming that Dewey was the first to highlight the "cyclical nature" of a "three-step process" concerned with the relationship between experience and education (Priest & Gass, 1997, p. 144). In his original text, Dewey described this process in the following way:

(1) observation of surrounding conditions; (2) knowledge of what has happened in similar situations in the past, a knowledge obtained partly by

recollection and partly from the information, advice, and warning of those who have had a wider experience; and (3) judgment which puts together what is observed and what is recalled to see what they signify. (Dewey, 1938, pp. 68–69)

In approaching this process, Dewey (1938, p. 69) emphasizes the educational importance of "procuring the postponement of immediate action upon desire until observation and judgment have intervened." This sentiment, along with other elements of Dewey's writing, has largely been interpreted to mean that "reflection" should follow "experience" as two steps in a sequence (Wurdinger & Paxton, 2003). This 'learning sequence' has become axiomatic in the literature. In one popular 1985 book on reflection, for instance, David Boud, Rosemary Keough, and David Walker proclaimed that "experience alone is not the key to learning" (p. 7). As stated earlier, Laura Joplin (1981) argued for a similar idea in her spiral-like model of experience, writing that "experience alone is insufficient to be called experiential education, and it is the reflection process which turns experience into experiential education" (p. 17). Instead of being seen as a form of experience itself, reflection came to be treated as some other kind of cognitive phenomenon occurring "in the privacy of one's own head" (Horwood, 1989). This experience-reflect sequence became firmly cemented in David Kolb's highly influential book *Experiential Learning: Experience as the Source of Learning and Development* (1985), which effectively canonized the 'experiential learning cycle' as the dominant model underpinning much of outdoor education (Seaman, 2008).

But here we would like to highlight a crucial point that problematizes some of this thinking on experiential learning. Dewey focused throughout his writing on reflection not as a thing in itself, not as a step in the learning process *after* experience, but as *one mode of experience*. He called this mode "reflective experience" (1916a, p. 177). As an advocate of scientific method, he of course emphasized the significance of careful, systematic thinking to modern education and learning; the problem is that, especially with the wide uptake of experiential learning cycles, experience *per se* has come to be understood primarily as 'doing,' hence separable from – and usually inferior to – reflection (see Michelson, 1999).

This is not Dewey's position and it leads to an unfortunate misunderstanding of his concept of *experience,* reducing it simply to a participatory exercise before the all-important task of reflection; hence the common emphasis on *method* within experiential reforms. For Dewey – a staunch pragmatist – there is no way to escape experience in order to reflect on it (seemingly from a non-experiential position sitting outside the original experience). Thus, to stop what Wichmann (1980) called the "process-centered syndrome," or the preoccupation with method that experiential learning models have tended to propagate, it is necessary to address what Dewey meant by reflective experience and its relationship to another mode of experience: *aesthetic experience.* For Dewey, awareness of how these two modes of experience operate, and what each one's role is with respect to *learning*, was to be the starting point for a unified theory of education. It is also instructive as to the potential role of outdoor education in a broader vision for schooling.

EXPERIENCE AS REFLECTIVE AND AESTHETIC

Across various texts, Dewey expends substantial effort communicating the importance of *reflective experience*, a phrase implying that reflection *is* experience. Reflective experience is both a common process everyone goes through on a routine basis, and an important way of being that can be cultivated to yield new personal and social knowledge – or, more precisely, to advance a scientific outlook on a constantly evolving world.

Two forms of reflective experience are basic to how people approach their lives. The first, what Dewey calls "the method of trial and error" (1916a, p. 169), involves proportionately less deliberate thinking, while the second involves more intentional, focused mental effort. In the first, firsthand activity dominates thinking, while in the second, cognitive activity dominates and controls how one approaches a problem or task. In trial and error, "we simply do something and when it fails, we do something else, and keep on trying until we hit upon something which works" (pp. 169–170). The incidental reflection that naturally occurs during this process enables us to see "*that* a certain way of acting and a certain consequence are connected, but we do not see *how* they are" (p. 170). The trial and error method is thus reflective experience in one sense, involving a basic level of thought, but in this mode one is thoroughly preoccupied with 'doing.' Importantly, Dewey was not disparaging the trial-and-error process here but merely specifying an aspect of how we deal with many routine problems we encounter on an everyday basis. Imagine if you had to pause and contemplate the reasoning behind your action each time you needed to solve a minor problem, how laborious life would be!

The second type of reflective experience is distinguished from trial and error by containing proportionately more analytic thought and is the type of reflective experience that is usually considered reflection *per se*. In this mode, it can be said that thinking dominates firsthand activity by making it an object of thought. This more analytic type is easiest to discern through a more comprehensive description of "the general features of reflective experience" that Dewey (1916a, p. 176) provides in *Democracy and Education*. These general features are:

(i) perplexity, confusion, doubt, due to the fact that one is implicated in an incomplete situation whose full character is not yet determined; (ii) a conjectural anticipation – a tentative interpretation of the given elements, attributing to them a tendency to effect certain consequences; (iii) a careful survey (examination, inspection, exploration, analysis) of all attainable consideration which will define and clarify the problem in hand; (iv) a consequent elaboration of the tentative hypothesis to make it more precise and more consistent, because squaring with a wider range of facts; (v) taking one stand upon the projected hypothesis as a plan of action which is applied to the existing state of affairs: doing something overtly to bring about the anticipated result, and thereby testing the hypothesis. (Dewey, 1916a, p. 176)

While these five features seem to present a simplistic cycle, Dewey was actually offering a deeper framework in which to relate the two types of reflective experience. In this account, the trial and error method (involving parts ii and v) includes more "incidental reflection" (1929a, p. 6), the other (iii and iv) being a more "regulated reflective inquiry" (p. 7). Dewey (1916a, p. 176, italics in original) acknowledges this distinction when he claims that "it is the extent and accuracy" of the features emphasized at "three and four [iii and iv] which mark off a distinctive reflective experience from one on the trial and error plane. They make *thinking* itself into an experience." In other words, thinking is distinguished from other activities only by deliberately emphasizing points iii and iv above – consciously working to define the problem at hand and develop hypothetical solutions. Crucially, this is experience of a certain kind – it is not something that comes *after* experience, but is rather a form of practical activity in its own right.

This does not mean diligent problem solving doesn't occur in trial and error. There, thinking involves "a conjectural anticipation – a tentative interpretation of the given elements, attributing to them a tendency to effect certain consequences," combined with "taking one stand upon the projected hypothesis as a plan of action which is applied to the existing state of affairs: doing something overtly to bring about the anticipated result, and thereby testing the hypothesis" (Dewey, 1916a, p. 176). The emphasis is not on abstract reflection, but on thinking within the concrete elements of the situation. We want to keep doing what we were doing (method) without having to *really* stop and think, so we only put minimal effort into thought. This means that if our first plan of action doesn't work – if it was pursued in error – we quickly shift gears and try another option until something works. Conversely, the second, more analytic mode of reflective experience would make the problem *and* our way of thinking about it an object of thought (subject matter), changing the character of the situation into one less preoccupied with *doing* and more dominated by *thinking.* At no point, though, do we become disconnected from experience.

Our point here is to show that action and reflection are not opposed but can be encapsulated in *one* of the modes of experience Dewey described: *reflective experience.* It is an error to separate out 'experience' from 'reflection' as two distinct phenomena. In fact, Dewey identified this as the root of the method/subject matter confusion: "reflection upon experience gives rise to a distinction of *what* we experience (the experienc*ed*) and the experienc*ing* – the *how*" (1916a, p. 196). And "when we give names to this distinction we have subject matter and method as our terms" (p. 196). But this distinction is not a division; it is not dualistic. Instead, *both* are aspects of a unified reality, present in all forms of experience from the most authoritarian classroom situation to the most gleeful outdoor excursion, from an engrossing hands-on task to a moment of private circumspection. In this conceptual framework, method and subject matter are always unified in 'real time' human experience, and one can tease them apart only for academic purposes.

For Dewey, there is nothing that could be called 'merely doing' and another that could be called 'purely thinking,' as if they are separable. In all experience, doing and thinking are what philosophers call *dialectically related*: doing one necessarily involves and transforms the other. As Dewey wrote, "we never get wholly beyond the trial and error situation. Our most elaborate and rationally consistent thought has to be tried in the world and thereby tried out" (1916a, p. 177). Even regulated reflection – the most 'abstract' form – cannot be disconnected from whatever problem is at hand. Practical problems frame reflective activity, and any hypotheses formulated in the mind must be subjected to trial and error in practice. It is therefore pointless to pit 'experience' and 'reflection' against one another, position them in any kind of sequence, or proclaim the alignment of 'method' to one and 'subject matter' to the other.

Dewey was also acutely aware of the cognitive bias that could arise if one overly valued and emphasized reflective experience – especially in its more focused, abstract form – as educators tend to do. As we pointed out, reflective experience always involves the interplay between trial and error and analytic reflection, even though one of these might predominate at any given time. But, if we took this kind of mental activity to be the entirety of experience and attempted to extrapolate a theory of curriculum from it, we would end up with a barren educational landscape (where, probably, battles between method and subject matter would rage!). To overcome this bias, one needs to turn to a key feature within Dewey's theory that we have not yet touched on significantly: *aesthetic experience.* To approach this mode of experience, we will carefully back our way out of reflective experience, as aesthetic experience is a very different mode of experience. Importantly, however, both are modes of experience: they are inherently connected.

Dewey (1916a, p. 176) argues that the origin of issues on which to reflect – problems that trigger reflective experience, in other words – is found in "perplexity, confusion, doubt, due to the fact that one is implicated in an incomplete situation whose full character is not yet determined." Elsewhere he argues: "all reflective inquiry starts from a problematic situation" (1929b, p. 189). If "no problem or difficulty in the quality of the experience has presented itself to provoke reflection," then "inquiry does not take place at all" (1903, p. 11). Here Dewey is pointing to the crucial role played by emotion and feeling in generating doubt, and its resolution, *knowing* (or, in pragmatic terms, *warrantability*). In a further account of reflective experience, in the second edition of *How We Think*, he points out that "the two limits of every unit of [reflective] thinking are a perplexed, troubled or confused situation at the beginning and a cleared-up, unified, resolved situation at the close" (1933, p. 106). He labels the beginning situation as *pre-reflective* and the resolved situation as *post-reflective.* Thus a "*pre*-reflective" situation "sets the problem to be solved; out of it grows the question that reflection has to answer" (pp. 106–107). And when "the doubt has been dispelled," then "the situation is *post*-reflective" (p. 107). The post-reflective situation involves "a direct experience of mastery, satisfaction, enjoyment" (p. 107). What Dewey is explaining here is that reflective experience occupies only part of our existence and that emotions – usually considered as the affective domain – act as a 'pivot' into reflective experience. But what is going on outside of reflective experience?

Dewey's pre-reflective and post-reflective categorizations point to reflective experience as emerging from and returning to a *different mode of experience* which is "non-reflective" in nature (1916b, p. 137fn). For Dewey, reflective experience is analogous to cognitive experience, and "cognitive experience must originate within that of a non-cognitive [non-reflective] sort" (1929b, p. 23). This is not to separate thinking from doing as 'experiential learning cycles' seem to have done; sadly, we fear that Dewey's choice of 'non-cognitive' as a descriptor has taken on a pejorative meaning in educational circles. He seemed to be aware of the potential for bias even in his own description:

> A typical illustration of what I mean by such non-cognitive experiences is found in my not infrequent statements to the effect that the assumption of the ubiquity of cognitive experience inevitably results in disparagement of things experienced by way of love, desire, hope, fear and other traits characteristic of human individuality. (Dewey, 1939, p. 548)

It is easy to mistake Dewey's discussions about cognitive and non-cognitive experience to mean that educators should create designs that emphasize reflection over non-cognitive or 'mere' doing. But Dewey moved beneath this debate with his work on what he called *aesthetic experience*, which is non-reflective in the sense that it describes our immediate feeling of a situation. We only apply labels to this immediate emotional sense – like love, desire, hope, and fear – in retrospect (reflectively). As Dewey (1934a, p. 42) explains, "experience is emotional but there are no separate things called emotions in it." When understood in this integrative way "emotion is the moving and cementing force" (p. 42) in experience. "It selects what is congruous and dyes what is selected with its color, thereby giving qualitative unity to materials externally disparate and dissimilar. It thus provides unity in and through the varied parts of an experience" (p. 42). Through his description of non-cognitive, emotion-laden experience, he arrives at his pivotal concept: "when the unity is of the sort already described, the experience has aesthetic character" (p. 42).[1]

Again, it is important to remember that Dewey's overriding theoretical aim was to express "the idea that there is an intimate and necessary relation between the processes of actual experience and education" (1938, p. 20). He was not arguing prescriptively that educators should insert more love, more desire, more hope, or more fear into their curriculum or classroom, or focus more on emotions and less on thinking. He was arguing that philosophers of education needed to *recognize* the significance of emotion in all human experience, including those that take place in situations we call 'educational' where 'knowing' is an ultimate goal. In recognizing the role emotion plays in thinking, the barren educational landscape would begin to have some color, texture, and climate – to approximate human experience in other domains; in other words, something schools notoriously failed to do.

Moreover, Dewey was careful to note that it wasn't as if schools were places where aesthetic experience *didn't* happen – it was just that teachers weren't generally concerned with the aesthetic experience of young people, so the aesthetic experience they helped create for children in school was often demotivating, coercive, and de-humanizing – emotionally negative – seemingly to forward the purpose of learning. As he wrote in *Experience and Education:*

> … the general pattern of school organization (by which I mean the relation of pupils to one another and to the teachers) constitutes the school as a kind of institution sharply marked off from other social institutions. Call up in imagination the ordinary school-room, its time-schedules, schemes of classification, of examination and promotion, of rules of order, and I think you will grasp what is meant by 'pattern of organization.' If then you contrast this with what goes on in the family, for example, you will appreciate what is meant by the school being a kind of institution sharply marked off from any other form of social organization. (1938, pp. 17–18)

Dewey wanted philosophers and educators to recognize that all of our experience in the world is aesthetic in nature, with people occasionally needing to switch into one or the other reflective mode when they perceive a "breakdown" in the flow of events (Koschmann, Kuutti & Hickman, 1998). Thus even reflective experience has its aesthetic qualities. "Esthetic cannot be sharply marked off from intellectual experience since the latter must bear an esthetic stamp to be itself complete" (Dewey, 1934a, p. 38). Curriculum theorists and school designers made one or more of several key mistakes related to this reality: (1) treating aesthetic experience as inferior to reflective experience when it comes to learning; (2) assuming it was unimportant in or could be programmed out of schooling; or (3) denying its existence at all by focusing exclusively on subject matter in the abstract, and making this the basis for how schools are organized. Conversely, Dewey was critical of progressives who made too much of children's emotions as if they could be understood apart from the substance of subject matter. Progressives were guilty of making "the child's present powers and interests as something finally significant in themselves" (1902b, p. 15). "Interests in reality," he wrote, "are but attitudes toward possible experiences; they are not achievements; their worth is in the leverage they afford, not in the accomplishment they represent" (p. 15). His challenge to educators was both to design situations with rich and meaningful emotional possibilities and to interpret children's interests as steps in the development of social attitudes and mastery of cultural knowledge.

Dewey advanced aesthetic experience as a key aspect of this project, seeing it as central to human life as it unfolds in real time and as the instigator to cultural innovation and growth. And in a typically non-dualistic way, Dewey identified a form of thinking that acknowledged aesthetic experience: what he called "affective thought" (1926, p. 3), or "qualitative thought" (1930, p. 18). This type of thinking can be understood as a kind of intuitive awareness of what is going on in an immediate sense – a 'feel for the game' one might say, or to borrow William Hanks's more technical phrasing, "a prereflective grasp of complex situations" involving masterful "timing of actions relative to changing circumstances: the ability to improvise" (Hanks, 1991, p. 20). Affective thought is distinct from more analytical reflection, which goes out of its way to isolate elements of a situation for close scrutiny in order to solve specific problems as they arise, or to categorize things in retrospect. In this sense aesthetic experience 'grounds' reflective experience; aesthetic experience is the earth from which reflective experience grows and continues to be rooted.

So aesthetic and reflective forms of thinking are both ongoing and necessary. Thus, rather than being the poor stepchild to reflective experience, disparaged for its inability to contribute much to learning, it is "to aesthetic experience" that "the philosopher must go to understand what experience is," Dewey (1934a, p. 274) claimed. By extension, any comprehensive – that is, non-confused – proposals for education must conceptualize the inherent relationship between the reflective and aesthetic modes of experience without arranging them in a hierarchy or a sequence. This would forever split apart doing, thinking, and feeling, and would be the perpetual source of confusion.

To further substantiate his claims, Dewey identified the historical origins of this tendency, a line of analysis that also laid a foundation for his radical conception of education. Here we take the reader through Dewey's observations about learning and schooling that reveal the historical roots of this separation of reflection from experience, and in turn offer a deeper understanding of his proposed way forward.

THE PROBLEM AND PROMISE OF LEARNING 'AS SUCH'

In his *My Pedagogic Creed*, Dewey wrote: "I believe that all education proceeds by the participation of the individual in the social consciousness of the [community]" (1897a, p. 77).[2] Notice Dewey did not say 'all education proceeds by *learning about* the social consciousness of the community,' as if he imagined a generation of hardworking Latin or civics students. He also did not say 'the *best type* of education occurs *when people participate* in the social consciousness of the community,' as if he was promoting 'experiential' over didactic teaching. Instead, he was advancing a basic existential fact: all education occurs through participation in historically formed, socially organized activities. What did he mean by this?

It will be useful to approach Dewey's position by revisiting his account of the somewhat haphazard rise of a familiar institution: schooling. Education as institutionalized mass schooling was only a relatively recent cultural invention in Dewey's day, and was, in his thinking, a largely ineffective form of participation in social consciousness. In a lecture titled *Waste in Education*, Dewey wrote: "from the standpoint of the child, the great waste in the school comes from his inability to utilize the experiences he gets outside the school in any complete and free way within the school itself" (1900, p. 89). He tells a story in a related essay, *The School and the Life of the Child,* of trying to find desks to equip his Chicago lab school. Running out of luck, he finally happens upon a shopkeeper who keenly observes, "I am afraid we have not what you want. You want something at which the children may work; these are all for listening" (p. 48). Dewey reflects on what this shopkeeper says:

> If we put before the minds eye the ordinary schoolroom, with its rows of ugly desks placed in geometrical order, crowded together so that there shall be as little moving room as possible, desks almost all of the same size, with just enough space to hold books, pencils, and paper, we can reconstruct the only educational activity that can possibly go on in such a place. (p. 48)

To identify more effective ways of educating than what is afforded in 'the ordinary schoolroom,' Dewey looked for historical analogues. He concluded that individuals throughout human history had mainly been 'educated' through direct involvement in the activities and traditions comprising community life, and only sporadically through formal instruction. Furthermore, education historically followed class lines; for most people it was 'informal,' a situation in which "subject matter is carried directly in the matrix of social intercourse. It is what the persons with whom an individual associates do and say" (Dewey, 1916a, p. 212). Most people throughout history did not participate in cultural activities in order to *learn,* they *learned* in order to participate more fully in cultural activities. For most, a specialized system of schooling such as the one Dewey describes above would have been an unwelcome distraction from meaningful participation in ordinary family, community, economic, and social life.

Dewey recognized that this fact could be grasped by looking back only a short time in the history of family, community, economic and social conduct. Here he is worth quoting at length:

> [Before] the factory system lies the household and neighborhood system. Those of us who are here today need go back only one, two, or at most three generations, to find a time when the household was practically the center in which were carried on, or about which were clustered, all the typical forms of industrial occupation. The clothing worn was for the most part made in the house; the members of the household were usually familiar also with the shearing of the sheep, the carding and spinning of the wool, and the plying of the loom. Instead of pressing a button and flooding the house with electric light, the whole process of getting illumination was followed in its toilsome length from the killing of the animal and the trying of fat to the making of wicks and dipping of candles. The supply of flour, of lumber, of foods, of building materials, of household furniture, even of metal ware, of nails, hinges, hammers, etc., was produced in the immediate neighborhood, in shops which were constantly open to inspection and often centers of congregation.

The entire industrial process stood revealed, from the production on the farm of the raw materials till the finished article was actually put to use. Not only this, but practically every member of the household had his own share in the work. The children, as they gained in strength and capacity, were gradually initiated into the mysteries of the several processes. It was a matter of immediate and personal concern, even to the point of actual participation. ... In all this there was continual training of observation, of ingenuity, constructive imagination, of logical thought, and of the sense of reality acquired through first-hand contact with actualities. The educative forces of the domestic spinning and weaving, of the sawmill, the gristmill, the cooper shop, and the blacksmith forge, were continuously operative. (Dewey, 1899, p. 457)

Here Dewey is not sentimentally bemoaning the loss of rural simplicity, but rather describing how most education in pre-industrial times was one and the same as learning and developing through firsthand participation in communal life; it was not set apart from that life the way school is, and it did not emphasize learning as a special activity one needed to practice on its own. All the necessary mental operations and dispositions were cultivated through participation. The organizing principles of education under those conditions were none other than carrying out everyday routines in pursuit of goals shared by mature members of the community. In other words, there was no 'curriculum' requiring special child-centered methods or an infusion of subject matter – only the shared labor of jointly pursuing family, neighbourhood, or workplace goals.

What was important for children to learn under these conditions 'stood revealed' and did not require focused instruction by an expert to interpret. As children 'grew in strength and capacity,' that is, as they developed the ability to contribute in increasingly valuable ways, they were 'gradually initiated' into new responsibilities and new roles. The test of learning lay in one's ability to meet these responsibilities and help make life run smoothly. So sequestering children in separate buildings with same-age peers made little sense, as there they neither learned from mature members of the community nor contributed to the community's overall wellbeing by sharing in its work.

Such was mass education before the 'factory system,' and much of what people needed to learn happened in that informal fashion. There were, however, certain aspects of community life that needed direct instruction since they were less explicitly revealed in everyday routines. Based on his observation of the routines that existed within informal education as described above, Dewey extrapolated to formal educational activities:

This fact [that most education happened informally] gives a clew to the understanding of the subject matter of formal or deliberate instruction. A connecting link is found in the stories, traditions, songs, and liturgies which accompany the doings and rites of a[n indigenous] social group.[2] They represent the stock of meanings which have been precipitated out of previous experience, which are so prized by the group as to be identified with their conception of their own collective line.... Even more pains are consciously taken to perpetuate the myths, legends, and sacred verbal formulae of the group than to transmit the directly useful customs of the group just because they cannot be picked up, as the latter can be in the ordinary processes of association. (Dewey, 1916a, pp. 212–213)

What Dewey is saying here is that only certain aspects of culture were subject to separate processes of 'learning.' Directly useful customs – or, in today's language, what children need to know and be able to do – could be 'picked up' through 'ordinary processes of association.' The expansion of commerce in the 16th century, for instance, which gave rise to primary schooling, required that more people learn to 'read, write, and compute.' But still "the aim was distinctly a practical one; it was utility, getting command of these tools, the symbols of learning, *not for the sake of learning*, but because they gave access to careers in life otherwise closed" (Dewey, 1900, p. 82, emphasis added). Even when people learned these new operations in a formal setting, learning still happened in the service of practical goals, not for its own sake.

Certain other aspects of communal life that did require focused instruction were not immanently useful to most people, and their acquisition was typically a function of both occupation and social class. What may be called high culture was a particular area 'worthy of taking conscious pains to perpetuate' where 'myths, legends, and sacred verbal formulae' were deemed to require focused instruction of some form. Moreover, not everyone needed intimate acquaintance with these traditions; religious authorities, for example, were the only ones who really required a deep understanding of rites and rituals in order to perform their social roles and maintain their power. Such high status knowledge was therefore both specialized and limited to a class of the population trained to operate in the realm of 'theory.' Only those chiefly responsible for managing symbolic and high status knowledge had to engage, in Dewey's terms, in specialized "training for the profession of learning" (1899, p. 466) – that is, in systematic, formal instruction.

Again, Dewey was not sentimentalizing this educational arrangement nor was he glorifying one or the other class of persons engaged in 'informal' versus 'formal' education. He was using historical analysis to point out some of the key forces shaping modern conceptions of education in the industrial era. This line of analysis revealed several important insights. For one, he showed that the way learning occurs culturally aligns with the overall societal division of labor, as well as the material aspects of people's existence. In pre-industrial times, there was little geographical mobility or movement between social classes; it would have made little sense for people to train for things that didn't help them pursue their practical goals since they probably couldn't surpass their social standing anyways. For another, he argued that mental operations did not develop in a vacuum but in the carrying out of one's job and according to one's evolving social roles. For most, this meant manual work, while for a select few it meant mental work; the historical fact was the same for both, but, crucially, only the latter were preoccupied with the work of 'learning.' For those who were educated 'informally,' learning served the goal of being productive in practical areas; for those educated 'formally,' learning *was* the goal. Hence Dewey called their activity "learning *as such*" (1900, p. 41, emphasis added).

The significance of Dewey's insights here cannot be overstated, as he characterizes learning as a *socially organized activity* and not only a psychological process. Mastering abstract concepts for their own sake was hardly a widespread concern; it was simply irrelevant to all but a few people. In pre-industrial times, and even in the early 20th century, the activity of *learning* aligned with people's life paths, which were largely predetermined by social class and societal function. The idea that everyone needed to learn because learning, in and of itself, is important did not yet exist at any wide scale (if one wasn't troubled by the prevailing social order, there were no problems with learning at all!). Thus, in Dewey's analysis, "the separation of theory and practice" mapped precisely onto "the division into 'cultured' people and 'workers'" (1900, p. 42). Significantly for our discussion here, this also means that formal education was the cultural institution that took *learning* as its exclusive preoccupation, and with the advent of compulsory schooling came the expectation that learning would become everybody's main activity, whether it aligned with their goals or not.

Enter Modern Times: Industrial-era Schooling. Dewey had skilfully shown that learning *as such* was a historically evolved, practical human activity and not merely a naturally occurring, psychological phenomenon; it especially was not a simple matter of storing up abstract facts or developing critical thinking skills outside of a specific setting. *Education,* then, was the cultural practice of organizing and distributing opportunities to learn in order to reproduce or transform the division of labor in society. In industrial society, this included helping people decide their own individual paths since they were no longer bound to traditional forms of work. Dewey, of course, saw in modern, mass education the potential to achieve political democracy and individual flourishing to an unprecedented degree. But even this potential did not emerge exclusively from the Enlightened minds of social reformers; it too was a function of historical processes. Speaking of the habit of mind he referred to as "experimental intelligence," Dewey wrote (with John L. Childs):

> ... it cannot be established *within* education except as the activities of the latter are founded on a clear idea of the active social forces of the day, of what they are doing, of their effect, for good and harm, upon values, and except as this idea and ideal are acted upon to direct experimentation in the currents of social life that run outside the school and that condition the educational meaning of whatever the school does. (1933, p. 319, emphasis in original)

For Dewey, education was not simply the process whereby individuals acquired academic content or developed along their own unique paths: it was a social institution that was uniquely able to advance political democracy, scientific progress, and individual possibilities. By the time he wrote *Experience and Education* in 1938, however, the opportunity for education to serve as an agent of social planning was losing ground to a destructive and unyielding form of capitalism. After witnessing vast social problems firsthand in the Great Depression, Dewey understood the power of capitalism to turn knowledge against democratic interests. Regarding "the economic and social problems of present society" (1938, p. 80), he wrote:

> They are products to a very large extent of the application of science in production and distribution of commodities and services, while the latter processes are the most important factor in determining the present relations of human beings and social groups to one another. (1938, p. 80)

Four decades earlier Dewey had urged reformers to see education "as part and parcel of the whole social evolution, and, in its more general features at least, as *inevitable*" (1900, p. 21, emphasis added). He understood that the combination of industrial capitalism and liberal democracy on a mass scale led naturally to the problem of how to organize *learning* so as to harness innovation, manage rapidly changing conditions across vast geographical distances, and prevent civilization from devolving into some disastrous form of social Darwinism. Under these historical conditions it was 'inconceivable' to him that education would not be fundamentally transformed from earlier cultural models, and much to his chagrin in 1938, the school was still approaching its role haphazardly and on the basis of mistaken thinking.

Like other social reformers of his day, Dewey was critical of aspects of capitalism and saw education as a way to redirect its negative consequences – a fact that earned him a reputation as a communist in some circles (see Dewey, 1934b). But unlike other socially critical progressives, such as George Counts (1932), Dewey's approach to school reform was to not propose new curriculum content or instructional methods but to focus on the cultural-historical nature of *learning*. Until people understood learning for what it was – a form of practical activity that historically has followed class lines – schools would be impotent to change society for the better or even to fulfil their promise of individual flourishing. As he wrote in *The School and Social Progress*:

> At present, the impulses which lie at the basis of the industrial system are either practically neglected or positively distorted during the school period. Until the instincts of construction and production are systematically laid hold of in the years of childhood and youth, until they are trained in social directions, enriched by historical interpretation, controlled and illuminated by scientific methods, we certainly are in no position even to locate the source of our economic evils, much less to deal with them effectively. (Dewey, 1900, pp. 38–39)

Dewey recognized that the principal mistake of the schools was making the "mediæval conception of learning" (1900, p. 41) – that is to say, formal instruction serving a highly specific cultural function, involving a narrow group of individuals, and devoted wholly to the mastery of abstract concepts – the model for "the

'New Education'" (p. 20). Schools were therefore woefully out of step with social conditions as they evolved under industrial capitalism and political democracy. Reformers had lost track of the historical context in which learning had expanded and had become preoccupied with technical questions of subject matter, which drove administration and methods of instruction. "This is the plane upon which it is too customary to consider school changes" (p. 20), he wrote, frustrated by their failure to understand learning as a fundamentally social and historical activity. "It is as rational to conceive of the locomotive or telegraph as personal devices" (p. 20). On this, it is again worth quoting Dewey at length:

> If we go back a few centuries, we find a practical monopoly of learning. The term *possession* of learning was, indeed, a happy one. Learning was a class matter. This was a necessary result of social conditions. There were not in existence any means by which the multitude could possibly have access to intellectual resources. These were stored up and hidden away in manuscripts. Of these there were at best only a few, and it required long and toilsome preparation to be able to do anything with them. A high-priesthood of learning, which guarded the treasury of truth and which doled it out to the masses under severe restrictions, was the inevitable expression of these conditions. But, as a direct result of the industrial revolution of which we have been speaking, this has been changed. Printing was invented; it was made commercial. Books, magazines, papers were multiplied and cheapened. As a result of the locomotive and telegraph, frequent, rapid, and cheap intercommunication by mails and electricity was called into being. Travel has been rendered easy; freedom of movement, with its accompanying exchange of ideas, indefinitely facilitated. The result has been an intellectual revolution. *Learning has been put into circulation.* While there still is, and probably always will be, a particular class having the special business of inquiry in hand, a distinctively learned class is henceforth *out of the question.* It is an anachronism. Knowledge is no longer an immobile solid; *it has been liquefied.* It is actively moving in all the currents of society itself. (1900, pp. 39–40, most emphases added)

A positive feature of modern industrial capitalism, which Dewey acknowledged, is that it had drastically changed people's relationship to knowledge; it made *becoming a knowing person* broadly available as a mode of living, with 'learning *as such*' a now-widespread activity that would enable growth in new directions. Thus the democratic ideal for *education* was to facilitate participation in the activity of learning as broadly and effectively as possible, opening up unprecedented pathways for individual and societal development. Dewey's eternal optimism in this regard is what made him so staunchly committed to democracy. A main challenge was therefore to construct institutions that engaged children in learning while still respecting its foundation in human history and material society. Viewed in this way, the method/subject matter debates that have dominated education for a century look particularly myopic, and it is easy to see how Dewey became exasperated by them.

Dewey never got the national conversation he wanted. Education – now entrenched as factory-model schooling – was being most profoundly shaped on the one hand by industrialists who wanted a flexible workforce, and on the other hand by traditional educators who wanted to distribute the fixed body of knowledge they saw as most important. By Dewey's analysis, *both* failed to understand the cultural significance of education and were therefore guilty of making 'the medieval conception of learning' the design template for modern education. And, since reformers largely used their same concepts to engage in the debate, they would never effect lasting change.

The pernicious dualisms Dewey argued against were historical artefacts of 'the medieval conception of learning' that had come to dominate modern educational consciousness and school design. Hence Dewey's insistence in 1938 on discovering *what education is.* The various forms of outdoor education throughout the 20th century have all, perhaps unwittingly, wrestled with but not solved this basic problem of *what education is,* and they have thus formed an uneasy but steady relationship with the 'medieval conception of learning,' which has at its core the dualisms we've focused on in this book.

KNOWING, DOING AND BEING

In the first section of this chapter, we explained Dewey's idea of *modes of experience,* including reflective and aesthetic experience. We also pointed out how educators tend to possess a strongly favourable bias toward 'cognitive' experience – whether that be of the trial and error (emphasizing doing) or more abstract (emphasizing knowing) type – and against 'non-cognitive' experience, a false dichotomy Dewey was keen to overcome by emphasizing the importance of *aesthetic* experience as non-reflective. One way this goal can be approached is by reimagining the relationship between *knowing, doing* and *being.* Here knowing and doing can be understood as analogous to subject matter and method (as *what* and *how* in Dewey's terms); these are the two types of reflective experience. Non-reflective aesthetic experience, on the other hand, is where we dwell – it is our life in an immediate and holistic emotional sense, aptly described as the way we are *being* a person, then and there.

Given his historical understanding of learning as outlined above, it is possible to see how Dewey took *knowing* to be a type of conduct, a form of practical human activity, a way of being a person. By the time of his writing at the turn of the 20th century, more people had become engaged in this activity than ever before, and education was positioned to expand participation even further – a prospect Dewey relished because of its democratic potential. Seen this way, it is possible to extend his conceptual framework and consider *a knowing person* to be a type of identity (here we are engaging in a reflective appreciation of the aesthetic experience of being a person in a certain way), one that has been most available among people engaged specifically in what Dewey called 'the profession of learning.' Historically, elites did the 'knowing' and everybody else did the 'doing,' but with mass education, this could potentially change. There is an important theoretical insight here: one can see again through Dewey's historical analysis that the doing/knowing dichotomy is a false distinction; *being* a student in a modern school involves *doing knowing* – or at least pretending to 'do knowing.' That is, modern education is organized to help people participate (or perhaps exclude them from participation) in the social activity of knowing, of being a knower, what used to be the province of elites.

What does it take to be a knower? To be good at it, you need not only demonstrate facility with abstract ideas, but adopt a favourable disposition to the cultural activity of *learning as such*: to make it part of who you are. In schools, this kind of person is highly regarded as an exemplary, motivated student. Outside of schools, Dewey was quick to point out that being a knower occupies comparatively little time in people's lives compared to the various other ways of being. For professional *know-ers*, like your humble authors, perhaps it occupies more time, life also consists of myriad other ways of being a person.

This line of analysis is crucial for understanding Dewey's philosophy, his designs for education, and how it can be employed to approach some of the main problems facing outdoor education and other reforms. It indicates that successful performance in all human activities is not separate from knowing: ways of doing inherently involve ways of knowing and vice-versa. Moreover, both are embedded within a way of being a person. Thus reflective thinking focused on knowing cannot be separated from that incidental reflection associated with continuing to do something, and both are integral to being a person in a certain way, as lived aesthetically. So, quite radically, Dewey's analysis actually means there is no such thing as *knowing* as a thing in itself. To be clear, Dewey is not disparaging the value of knowing as a mode of human activity – in fact doing *knowing* responsibly and ethically in modern society was an overriding concern of his – but that is how he wants us to think about it: as a form of activity and one that contributes to other forms of activity – as a way of doing things among the many ways of being a person.

Several dualisms dissolve through this line of analysis – outdoor/indoor, method/subject matter, and doing/thinking. These dualisms revolve around the two types of reflective experience, but dissolving them also requires an understanding of the connection between reflective and aesthetic experience. This means that one can *only* learn through participation in activity, through *experience* – understood as knowing doing *and* being – reflective *and* aesthetic, both in their unity; there simply is nothing else. So, the main question facing reformist outdoor educators is not the either/or choice between 'Is it a subject matter?' or 'Is it a method that is preferable to indoor alternatives?' Instead, this can be reconceived as an awareness of how outdoor activities are not only ways of doing, but they are indeed also ways of knowing – and even more than this, they are ways of being a person. The leading question for outdoor educators, then, is: '*what ways of being a person centrally involve the outdoors, and what does it take to knowledgeably participate in these activities?*'

This argument positions us to better understand what Dewey meant when he said, in the opening line of *My Pedagogic Creed* (1897, p. 77), "all education proceeds by participation in the social consciousness of the [community]." Or, in our phrasing, all education occurs through participation in historically formed, socially organized activities – including *learning.* Sadly, compulsory institutionalized schooling has forced everyone to participate in and identify with the activity of learning, conducted in a particularly narrow fashion, and whether or not it aligns with or informs their other ways of being.

Let us elaborate by turning to curriculum for a moment. *Knowing* as a broadly available type of activity is a relatively recent historical development (and, as an aside, an increasingly important identity to achieve in a 21st century 'information based' economy – see Wells & Claxton, 2002). Put in these terms, it becomes very easy to see how it is that schools are preoccupied with getting people to be *know-ers.* But schools make the terrible, paradoxical mistake of promoting the activity of *know-ing* and the identity of *the know-er* while at the same time disparaging the activity of *do-ing* and the identity of *do-er* – and therefore also ignoring, in the aesthetic sense, other ways of *be-ing* a person (think of the social status of vocational students in most high schools). Philosophically speaking, this is how the design of most modern schools rests on a faulty premise – it artificially opposes knowing and doing, and then bases even its most progressive reforms on one side or the other, while seemingly ignoring being. This not only systematically produces disaffection for many children, it also creates unresolvable curriculum design challenges that can only result in crowding.

When the focus is on *knowing* as a thing in itself, a main problem for the school is to decide on what is important to know and how to best organize this (subject matter and its scope and sequence in the curriculum), and then how best to get people to 'internalize' it (a matter of teaching methods, which come second) – all with the ill directed aim of preparing students for ways of being that are outside the realm of their experience. This invariably leads to disputes which focus primarily on subject matter: about what content is most valuable, how it builds on other content, how it relates to still more content, etc. Life is approached and ordered as if it were a knowledge sequence to be learned in the monochrome manner of being a student. Crucially, Dewey wanted educators to recognize how actual life (or *experience*) is more about how we develop through encountering various ways of being a person.

It is easy to see how such a focus on knowledge and knowing can quickly lead to crowding, as well as the frustration that children's interests and talents are constantly ignored. Add to this the desire to promote *do-ing,* as progressives have always done – including such activities as music, art, physical education, vocational training, outdoor recreation, play, and so on – and you have on your hands a major volume problem, especially as this 'doing' is mined for its subject matter and the area of interest is argued for as a subject (as has been shown with nature-study and outdoor education). Reforms can then only consist of supplanting existing areas or shrinking them so as to fit more of them in. Dewey described the problem in the following way:

> [The educational system] is more like a patchwork, and a patchwork whose pieces do not form a pattern. It is a patchwork of the old and the new; of unreconstructed survivals from the past and of things introduced because of new conditions.... In consequence, the new studies that have been introduced have split up the curriculum into unrelated parts and created congestion. There are too many studies and too many courses of study, and the result is confusion. (Dewey, 1935, p. 333)

Here we arrive at the crux of the matter, with a set of conceptual tools to better understand it: the perpetual existence of 'confusion' stems from the faulty preoccupation with *knowing* and *doing* as things-in-themselves, while simultaneously ignoring and omitting concern for *being*; the consequence is its inevitable organizational product *the crowded curriculum*. Based on this faulty premise, the logic of schooling proceeds as follows:

> There is a certain amount – a fixed quantity – of ready-made results and accomplishments to be acquired by all children alike in a given time. It is in response to this demand that the curriculum has been developed from the elementary school up through the college. There is just so much desirable knowledge, and there are just so many needed technical accomplishments in the world. Then comes the mathematical problem of dividing this by the six, twelve, or sixteen years of school life. Now give the children every year just the appropriate fraction of the total, and by the time they have finished they will have mastered the whole. (Dewey, 1900, p. 50)

If one approaches education as a matter of getting the right *balance* of knowing and doing (see Coleman, 1995), the questions of 'How to get more nature into the schools?' and 'How to get kids outdoors?' become important, a matter of values and choices; *if* people valued nature more, *then* they'd drop other things and spend more time on/in it. Or maybe they'd change how they're teaching a subject area – say, chemistry – so it can be done outside and not inside, and in a more engaging fashion. This is how outdoor education has evolved and it reflects a fairly standard approach to curriculum. It ultimately leaves all the dualisms intact, however, solving nothing and making 'outdoor education' no more central to schooling than home economics or algebra or the Scarlet Letter. This leads also to cycles of reform; it is just a matter of time before the champion of outdoor education moves on, the outdoor center becomes unaffordable, a new administrator with different values arrives and starts a new program, or external trends progress to where 'test prep' has to take over space in the curriculum. Of course, schools with 'nature' or 'the outdoors' or 'ecology' as part of their mission fare better than comprehensive schools, but do not resolve the systemic issue. We believe these cycles of reform have been, at root, plagued with the dualistic thinking Dewey tried to overcome. Central to his solution was the concept of occupations, importantly aligned with both aesthetic and reflective experience – as being, doing and knowing – to which we now turn.

SUMMARY

In this chapter we have covered a lot of ground, both philosophical and historical – though all, of course, to do with education and by implication outdoor education. We began by highlighting how the conception, commonly held in experiential learning circles, that experience and reflection, doing and thinking, are two different types of things (one experience and one not) is an erroneous position. We have shown this by going back to Dewey's own work in this area. Here Dewey refers to *reflective experience* as one mode of experience involving two types: type one is comparatively *less* reflective, which accentuates getting on with doing things – reflective thinking here is 'incidental' or 'trial and error' in that it grasps possible solutions without necessarily thinking them through in detail; type two is *more* reflective, and while in service of getting on with doing things, it can wander beyond the concrete situation in a more abstract pursuit of solutions – reflective thinking here is 'regulated.' In other words, reflection is not an addition to experience, it is itself experience. Reflection is both doing and knowing. This argument points to the intimate connections that exist between method and subject matter; these are connected in the same way: functionally in the pursuit of practical goals.

But this functional connection within reflective experience still does not fully provide a way out of the underlying confusion Dewey witnessed in education. While we can see that within reflective experience method and subject matter are connected, there must be something in experience which guides this connection. Here Dewey spoke of *aesthetic experience* as that mode of experience which reflection emerges from, to which it is always beholden, and to which it returns; or put in a better way: aesthetic experience underpins reflective experience.

Before embarking on a further exploration of the connection between reflective and aesthetic experience, the reader should understand in greater depth the historical roots to the confusion in education, and Dewey's perspective on this. Such a historical understanding signals the need for better comprehending the connection between reflective and aesthetic experience. Central to Dewey' historical perspective was the development of institutionalized schooling, which grew from the perceived need to formalize learning in those specialized and highly valued cultural activities that were usually outside of the everyday experiences of most community members. Dewey coined this 'the medieval conception of learning,' and it was this conception of learning that underpinned the development of school as an institution. Yet schools, so conceived, were not able to service the ideals of a democratic community, Dewey argued. Even reforms in education such as those around vocations considered to be more mundane (rather than those believed to be special and only open to the elite) became entrenched within this medieval conception of learning, with application of formalized forms of learning resulting in schools based on the efficient model of the factory.

The development of schooling in this way was premised on the belief that knowing is the most important aspect of education, more important than doing. Yet both Dewey's understanding of reflective experience and his historical observations related to learning and schooling have shown us that knowing is indeed a form of doing, and that it was separated from doing for cultural reasons rooted in class divisions. But Dewey's approach to the problem of confusion in education goes deeper than this – to aesthetic experience, that immediate and direct form of experience which is holistic in an emotional sense. Aesthetic experience is where we live – it is the way we are *being* a person, *here and now*. Armed with this understanding we are better placed to take the next step in presenting our argument. This next step involves addressing Dewey's notion of education through occupations, which are both aesthetic and reflective – being, doing and knowing in unity. As Miettinen (2006) points out, *work* was, for Dewey, the prototypical activity for understanding knowledge in reality. Dewey therefore looked to work activity as a foundation for effective and meaningful education: ,"education *through* occupations ... combines within itself more of the factors conducive to learning than any other method" (1916a, p. 361).

NOTES

[1] Dewey uses the spellings esthetic and aesthetic. We shall use aesthetic when it is in our own words but retain Dewey's spellings in quotes.

[2] We have deleted the term 'race' from this quote as, following Fallace (2012), we are sensitive to the difficulty surrounding Dewey's early use of this term. In its place we have employed the term 'community' which we believe more clearly conveys the pluralistic beliefs that came to characterize his thought.

[3] We have replaced the term 'primitive' with the term 'indigenous' so as to bring this aspect of Dewey's language use into a form of expression which more appropriately acknowledges the sophistication of indigenous cultures, a stance Dewey himself adopted later in his career (Fallace, 2012).

CHAPTER 6

LOOKING AHEAD: OUTDOOR EDUCATION
AS *OCCUPATION*

OCCUPATIONS AS PROGRESSIVE ORGANIZATION OF EDUCATION

We turn now to the way Dewey sought to positively apply his unified theory about reflective and aesthetic experience – expressed through *work activity* or *occupations* – in education. As we explained, when schooling is about knowing, the curricular project problematically becomes carving out and toting up subject matter on one side, figuring out at what age children are capable of acquiring it, and aligning this list with appropriate instructional methods on the other side. If the alignment goes well, students will presumably have "mastered the whole," as Dewey (1900, p. 50) said; if not, you might add a little more subject matter, rearrange it, or try different methods. It is beyond the scope of our book to go deeper into the numerous problems Dewey had with this form of planning, so we will skip to his solution: organizing learning as participation in *occupations.*

We want to stress upfront that Dewey's framework of *reflective experience* (in both trial and error and regulated senses) and *aesthetic experience* was meant to be descriptive. In other words, he wrote about these aspects of human existence from a philosophical standpoint and not as prescriptions for educational practice. He did not, for instance, believe that schools should emphasize regulative/reflective experience because aesthetic experience was somehow inferior and unable to adequately produce learning. And despite proclamations that reflective experience emerges from and returns to aesthetic experience, he did not mean that this needed to be facilitated by a teacher or had some kind of preordained order to it that could be 'programmed into' a lesson. Aesthetic and reflective experience are basic conditions of human existence. But, awareness of their relationship as well as their changing character over historical time was used by Dewey as a foundation for making prescriptions about how to organize education.

Dewey (1900, p. 78) describes "organization" as "nothing but getting things into connection with one another, so that they work easily, flexibly and fully." Organization in traditional education typically is not easy, flexible, or thorough. It usually occurs around subject matter: it is the bodies of knowledge, the disciplines as school subjects, that organize traditional education. If one assumes this logic to be 'natural,' it is easy to see why some have gone to great lengths to define outdoor education as a subject – it is the *lingua franca* of schooling and the legitimacy of any reform often depends on the ability to fit into the traditional mode of organization. We have already discussed the flaws Dewey saw in this approach.

Child-centered progressives also have an organizing framework, it is just based on a different logic. Progressive models of curriculum are achieved by arranging activities according to their supposed 'developmental appropriateness.' It is children's enthusiasm for certain activities at various stages of growth that directs organization, and in this framework outdoor education is viewed as a method for reaching children at certain points in time. Dewey also rejected this mode of organization because it paid insufficient attention to the larger social and historical contexts in which schools evolved and individuals developed. He wrote: "There is no such thing as sheer self activity possible – because all activity takes place in a medium, in a situation, and with reference to its conditions" (1902b, pp. 30–31). He would later sharpen this criticism by writing: "nothing can be more absurd educationally than to make a plea for a variety of active occupations in school while decrying the need for progressive organization of information and ideas" (1938, p. 84). Progressive reformers, in other words, had shirked their responsibility for gradually incorporating children into the complexities of social life through education, believing instead that children's personal activity choices were sufficient to direct organization.

As might be expected by now, Dewey's view of organization is complex and expansive. He argues that education consists of more than subject matter and methods, and includes the "trinity of ... subject matter, methods, and administration" (1916a, p. 193). By administration Dewey means more than setting policies and managing personnel; he means an underlying logic that determines the relationship among all aspects of the institution, and mirrors to some extent the way life is carried on socially. In this view it is not sufficient to see organization as revolving around subject matter as academic disciplines, or around methods as different kinds of engaging activities. In Dewey's view, the "moral trinity of the school" is:

1. the life of the school as a social institution in itself;
2. methods of learning and of doing work; and
3. the school studies or curriculum. (1909, p. 29)

Thus organization is rooted in something deeper than subject matter and method; in a non-trivial sense, the organization is the life of the school, and moreover, it must be based on connections between the school and larger community and social life, or as Dewey put it, connections that are inherent in the relationship between education and experience.

Dewey posed many challenging questions to progressive educators, and one of the most perplexing asks them to consider educational organization. He asks, "What is the place and meaning of subject matter and of organization *within* experience? How does subject-matter function? Is there anything inherent in experience which tends towards progressive organization of its contents?" (1938, p. 20). What we believe Dewey is urging here is the need to address a deeper sense of organization, a directing principle that involves subject matter (what is experienc*ed*) and method (how experienc*ing* occurs) not just in a two-part relationship, but underpinned by a deeper merging of these together as one – in the ways life has been lived aesthetically throughout human history.

To understand organization of experience as Dewey meant it, one must turn to aesthetic experience – which is where life happens for him. As we've stated, the important distinction between reflective and aesthetic experience lies in the emphasis on aesthetic experience as emotional in nature. Aesthetic experience is holistic, rather than concerned with understanding things as component parts (which is what reflective experience is concerned with). It offers "deep and abiding experience of the nature of fully harmonized experience" (Dewey, 1926, p. 9) and forms "the basis of an educational experience which counteracts the disrupting tendencies of the hard-and-fast specializations, compartmental divisions and rigid segregations which so confuse and nullify our present life." But if education is not organized around a discipline or body of knowledge (subject matter) or an activity (method), then what *does* provide such aesthetic unity in experience? For Dewey this living unity can be found in the concept of *occupations*, which Higgins (2005, p. 449) argues "opens onto [Dewey's] treatment of aesthetics." Dewey explained his understanding of the concept as follows:

> By occupation is not meant any kind of "busy work" or exercises that may be given to a child in order to keep him out of mischief or idleness when seated at his desk. By occupation I mean a mode of activity on the part of the child which reproduces, or runs parallel to, some form of work carried on in social life. (Dewey, 1915, p. 132)

Although Dewey viewed work activity as a prototype for understanding knowing and being, he uses the term occupation very broadly, beyond its usual meaning associated with adult jobs. An education through occupations is therefore not vocational education as we tend to understand it. Yet somehow it is the key to finding a way out of the educational confusion that we experience.

> Both practically and philosophically, the key to the present educational situation lies in a gradual reconstruction of school materials and methods so as to utilize various forms of occupation typifying social callings, and to bring out their intellectual and moral content. (1916a, pp. 368–369)

Gaining a well-informed sense for what Dewey meant by occupation is thus critical to understanding his position on education. Helping us with such an understanding are the functional connections he makes across aesthetic experience and the two types of reflective experience. Occupations thus contain three unified elements.

Firstly, occupations are aesthetic and therefore holistic. Such aesthetic holism includes what we usually distinguish as self, others and environment, but in an aesthetic way, as *immediately felt* – not reflected upon as separate parts. We have a felt sense of their oneness. Thus they are, in this aesthetic sense – or in the sense of *being* – different ways of living as a person in the social world, as, for instance, one would *be* a rock-climber, an artist, a doctor, or a sister. Such ways of being, as aesthetic wholes, always embrace others and environment (Quay, in press); they are not individualistic (but they can seem this way when considered reflectively). Hence being a rock-climber is a socially defined pursuit that involves *doing* certain things with others and environment, and *knowing* others and environment in specific ways. There is no sense of individualism (understood as separation from others or environment) in Dewey's understanding of occupations. "Active occupations," wrote Dewey (1916a, p. 232), are "concerned primarily with *wholes.*" And "wholes for purposes of education are not ... physical affairs. Intellectually the existence of a whole depends upon concern or interest; it is qualitative, the completeness of appeal made by a situation" (p. 232). Dewey is here drawing a direct connection between occupation and interest in this aesthetic way. Interest, for Dewey, did not simply signify a personal (as opposed to social) preference; interest is *not* merely personal, it is always social and environmental as well. In other words, interests, like occupations, can be understood as aesthetic experience. For teachers, interests are indicators as to the evolving, aesthetic experience of children; *points of departure* for the social activity of teaching.

Secondly, occupations are associated with doing. An occupation "is a continuous activity having a purpose" (1916a, p. 361). 'Continuous' here has both long- and short-term dimensions, meaning it possesses a history and direction that transcends any one person's involvement as well as being of such duration that it takes on a depth of meaning not possible with many short term affairs. For instance, it is those longer term occupations in our lives that tend to be the most meaningful: being a brother/sister, a father/mother, and one's longer term career callings. In an educational sense, occupation can, by this measure of activity, of doing, be equated with method.

Thirdly, an occupation has something to say about knowing. An occupation or "calling is ... of necessity an organizing principle for information and ideas; for knowledge and intellectual growth" (1916a, p. 362). It provides "an axis which runs through an immense diversity of detail" and thereby prompts "different experiences, facts, items of information to fall into order with one another" (p. 362). This has obvious ramifications for education in relation to subject matter. Traditionally, curriculum specialists have looked to subject matter to organize education. Dewey turns this prescription on its head and instead states that subject matter is itself organized by occupations.

In Dewey's formulation, *occupation* is the key unit of analysis, spanning and encompassing both aesthetic and reflective experience. It is aesthetic in its holistic nature, a holism that also contains Dewey's notion of interest. In connection with Dewey's account of reflective experience we have seen that occupation is, of course, activity, doing, and thus involving an incidental or trial and error form of reflection. In addition, an occupation supplies the organizing principle for knowledge, for subject matter. Education through occupations thereby gives shape and definition to *learning* in a way that 'learning as such' – meaning the disconnected, abstract, largely purposeless activity found in schools – does not; even though, historically, *learning* must also be understood as an occupation in its own right (an insight most teachers in schools fail to comprehend). So an occupation is much more than just a job or topic of study or a method for teaching; an occupation is a living aesthetic whole whose purpose and inherent structure organizes both doing (method) *and* knowing (subject matter). It thus became one of Dewey's core organizing principles for education (see figure 25).

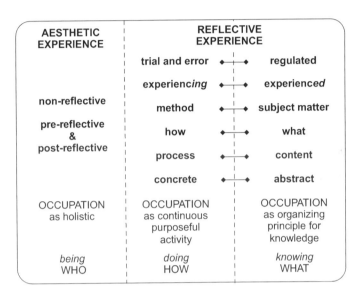

Figure 25. A portrayal of Dewey's modes of experience – aesthetic and reflective – as these align with his notion of occupations, thereby highlighting the connection between experience and education (through occupations).

But if Dewey's sense of occupation is so powerful, why has it not so far made the inroads into educational theory and practice?. One reason is because the term 'occupation' has caused problems over the years. Dewey (1916a, p. 360) often used the words "occupation," "vocation" and "calling" synonymously, yet his understanding of occupation is in stark contrast to that employed in vocational education as this was practiced in his day and is still practiced today. Dewey's (1915, p. 133) declaration that "occupation ... must ... be carefully distinguished from work which educates primarily for a trade" was an extremely difficult sell, going against the grain of a popular understanding that remains with us in contemporary vocational education. The issue for Dewey was the problematic interpretation of occupations as adult jobs which could be trained for specifically, a prevailing tendency that turned schools into handmaidens to industry. In contrast to this, he saw a "right occupation" (1916a, p. 360) as an aesthetic whole in which one's self is meaningfully embedded amongst others and environment such that all involved can grow and thrive. An occupation is thus 'right' when it gains significance in the context of the local group or community – which highlights the difference between the social worlds of most young people and adult jobs – and it is thus educative as opposed to "mis-educative" (1938, p. 25).

So, equipped with an aesthetic understanding of occupations, Dewey saw the educational challenge as one "of utilizing the factors of industry to make school life more active, more full of immediate meaning, more connected with out-of-school experience" (1916a, p. 369). We stress again that Dewey was not using 'industry' here to reference adult jobs *as such*. His goal was "not that of making the schools an adjunct to manufacture and commerce" (p. 369). Rather occupations employed in education must leverage the interests and industries of the (always social) child, as well as orient these to increasingly complex and widening forms of mature, social activity. Just as in adult education, where the occupations in question are relevant to the adults concerned, so with school education: the occupations developed as the units of work that organize education should be relevant to the larger social purposes of the people for whom they are meant to be significant, including children and youth themselves. Educational occupations thus become "familiar occupations" (1900, p. 25) because young people have some understanding of them as they constitute their social lives.

In this way, occupations function as the building blocks of living. Dewey provided some examples of occupations that were significant for the children of his day:

> Outdoor excursions, gardening, cooking, sewing, printing, book-binding, weaving, painting, drawing, singing, dramatization, story-telling, reading and writing as active pursuits with social aims (not as mere exercises for acquiring skill for future use), in addition to countless variety of plays and games, designate some of the modes of occupation. (Dewey, 1916a, p. 230)

These examples are of occupations (relevant a century ago, but most still relevant for children today) that organize social life. At face, they might look like mere activities, or methods, but Dewey cautions that "it is not enough to introduce plays and games, hand work and manual exercises" (p. 230) as standalone activities or as gimmicks designed to capture attention. "Everything depends upon the way in which they [occupations] are employed" (p. 230). "The problem of the educator" is then "to engage pupils in these activities in such ways that while manual skill and technical efficiency are gained and immediate satisfaction found in the work, together with preparation for later usefulness, these things shall be subordinated to *education*," where education means, "to intellectual results and the forming of socialized disposition" (p. 231). For Dewey, subject matter was therefore a paramount concern, however subject matter is *always* only meaningful within an occupation – this is a true fact of both historical and individual (or "ontogenetic") development.

This three pronged understanding of occupation as being, doing, and knowing highlights the connection between occupations and Dewey's trinity of the school.

Not just as subject matter, nor merely as activities, occupations are more than this – they are organizing of life. As such, they should organize the life of the school:

> The great thing to keep in mind … regarding the introduction into the school of various forms of active occupation, is that through them the entire spirit of the school is renewed. It has a chance to affiliate itself with life, to become the child's habitat, where he learns through directed living; instead of being only a place to learn lessons having an abstract and remote reference to some possible living to be done in the future. (Dewey, 1900, pp. 31–32)

OCCUPATIONS AND SCHOOLING

Dewey examined schooling from the point of view of occupations, in both a critical and a constructive sense. From a critical perspective, the main occupation of schooling is being an academic student, a peculiar occupation that is *not* significant for many young people and certainly has few parallels in adult life (except as it serves adult work: see Beach, 1995). Dewey described the predictable consequences of this fact:

> Enforced quiet and acquiescence prevent pupils from disclosing their true natures. They enforce artificial uniformity. They put seeming before being. They place a premium on preserving the outward appearance of attention, decorum, and obedience. And everyone who is acquainted with schools in which this system prevailed well knows what thoughts, imaginations, desires, and sly activities ran their own unchecked course behind this façade. They were disclosed to the teacher only when some untoward act led to their detection.... Mechanical uniformity of studies and methods creates a kind of uniform immobility and this reacts to perpetuate uniformity of studies and recitations, while behind this enforced uniformity individual tendencies operate in irregular and more or less forbidden ways. (Dewey, 1938, p. 62)

Here we can see how enforcing the occupation of *being an academic student* leads to the development of other occupations designed to subvert it. In fact, research since Dewey's time has shown that, when children perceive being a student as meaningless, they become invested in 'seeming' to be knowing persons and 'sly activities' become prevalent, often yielding self-destructive results (see Eckert, 1989; Willis, 1977 for classic examples). Instead, Dewey wanted schools to provide more authentic and productive forms of occupation, like that found through participation in community activities that are meaningful to the young people involved.

Constructively designing schools around the aesthetic character of many significant occupations, instead of the one general occupation of being an academic student, opens up new possibilities for subject matter organization, for 'content' learned in one occupation can be meaningful in another. For example the subject matter of science is not only relevant when one is an academic student, or even a scientist. In fact much of the importance of the disciplines is gained from the broad possible application of their bodies of knowledge. This knowledge is applied in a meaningful way within other occupations, such as that of gardening.

> Gardening, for example, need not be taught either for the sake of preparing future gardeners, or as an agreeable way of passing time. It affords an avenue of approach to knowledge of the place of farming and horticulture have had … and which they occupy in present social organization. Carried on in an environment educationally controlled, they are means for making study of the facts of growth, the chemistry of soil, the role of light, air and moisture, injurious and helpful animal life, etc. There is nothing in the elementary study of botany which cannot be introduced in a vital way in connection with caring for the growth of seeds. Instead of the subject matter belonging to a peculiar study called botany, it will then belong to life, and will find, moreover, its natural correlations with the facts of soil, animal life, and human relations. (Dewey, 1916a, p. 235)

Dewey's argument is that knowledge is meaningfully embedded not only in mature disciplines, which tend to be the focus of specific adult occupations, but in other occupations relevant to children and young people that can be harnessed in education. Unlike both traditional and progressive reformers, who set subject matter and method in opposition, Dewey (writing with his daughter Evelyn) saw them as integrally related in the developing person's experience.

> The daily experiences of the child, his life from day to day, and the subject matter of the schoolroom, are parts of the same thing…. To oppose one to the other is to oppose the infancy and maturity of the same growing life; it is to set the moving tendency and the final result of the same process over against each other; it is to hold that the nature and the destiny of the child war with each other (Dewey & Dewey, 1915, p. 71).

When a unit of work is understood as an occupation – such as being a gardener – it is holistic in that the participants consider themselves to *be* gardeners, or seed growers, or some other malleable label that captures *who* they are being in an immediate aesthetic sense (in which others and environment are embedded). This can also be reflectively experienced as *how* they are doing things (method), and *what* they are knowing (subject matter). So aesthetically, being a gardener is the holistic way in which this occupation is lived; while reflectively, it is an identity that involves a particular arrangement of action and knowledge, method and subject matter. Thus 'occupation' is a preferable descriptor of an educational unit over *topic*, which tends to emphasize subject matter and omit the identity-conferring aspect of participation in social activity.

Importantly, we emphasize again that being a gardener understood in this aesthetic way is not meant as an individualistic pursuit – as if the educational unit is designed to cater to individuals. With reference to the perceived division between social and individual perspectives, Dewey describes "an occupation" as "the only thing which balances the distinctive capacity of an individual with his social service" (1916a, p. 360). In fact for Dewey an occupation is "any form of continuous activity which renders service to others and engages personal powers in behalf of the accomplishment of results" (p. 373). In this sense an occupation is a "form of social life" (p. 115). Occupations are always socially defined, even if individually salient; they cannot be understood outside of their social meaning.

Dewey (1916a, p. 373) summarizes his conception of occupation when he states, "education *through* occupations ... combines within itself more of the factors conducive to learning than any other method" (p. 361). Like agricultural activities at the turn of the 20th century, around which traditional life revolved, an occupation subordinates learning to the pursuit of meaningful goals that are valued by the community and relevant to the individual. The concept "calls instincts and habits into play; it is a foe to passive receptivity. It has an end in view; results are to be accomplished," for an occupation "appeals to thought; it demands that an idea of an end be steadily maintained, so that activity cannot be either routine or capricious" (p. 361). One need only think of the often profound learning that goes on in adult workplaces to realize how occupations inherently involve doing with purpose (which can be understood as method) as well as knowing (which draws on subject matter). Hence Dewey argues that "the *only* alternative to a reactionary return to the educational traditions of the past lies in working out the intellectual possibilities resident in various arts, crafts, and occupations, and reorganizing the curriculum accordingly" (1933, p. 217, emphasis added). Occupation, as here described, would eradicate method and subject matter dichotomies, finally rising to the challenge of providing a worthwhile education on a mass scale.

THE FUTURE OF (OUTDOOR) EDUCATION

The challenge Dewey poses for outdoor educators – really for all educators – is to see beyond the confusion between method and subject matter. The task is to imagine an education organized around occupations: socially meaningful units of cooperative work in which method and subject matter are inherently integrated and arranged carefully by teachers to "parallel ... some form of work carried on in social life" (Dewey, 1915, p. 132) as well as gain a reflective (scientific) understanding of the meaning of that work to self and society. If we take a closer look at schools, the official and primary occupation seems to be that of the academic student. What this means specifically will be different for each school subject set in a specific community, but there is a large degree of uniformity across institutions and subjects; being a math student is much like being a science student, which is much like being a language student, and so on (see Popkewitz, 2007; Säljö & Wyndhamm, 1993). In all cases, despite differences in subject matter, the goal is learning content for purposes of assessment, the chief identity available is that of *student,* and the work primarily involves producing things that eventually end up in a wastebasket.[1]

Doing and knowing in school, from a young person's perspective, are usually undertaken for the purpose of passing examinations; thus the nagging and age-old questions: 'When will I need to know this? Will this be on the test?' Adults like to argue that this academic doing and knowing is important to attaining a college degree or landing a job. This is true but only somewhat superficially. In reality, participating in the occupation of being a student is often directed towards a future that young people have difficulty understanding as a real part of their lives currently, or that progressively integrates them in meaningful ways into the social fabric of the broader community. So while acknowledging "that the future has to be taken into account at every stage of the educational process," Dewey (1938, p. 47) was also keenly aware that "this idea is easily misunderstood and is badly distorted in traditional education."

> Its assumption is, that by acquiring certain skills and by learning certain subjects which would be needed later (perhaps in college or perhaps in adult life) pupils are as a matter of course made ready for the needs and circumstances of the future. (Dewey, 1938, p. 47)

Hence Dewey (1938, p. 47) derided "'preparation'" in these terms as "a treacherous idea." This applies to vocational education as well, which, although perhaps clearer in its pathways to adult life, is still beholden to the notion of teaching skills and knowledge that gain their significance in an occupation existing in a presumed future which is not a part of the life of the young people involved. Dewey (1893, p. 660) revealed that if personally "asked to name the most needed of all reforms in the spirit of education," he "should say: 'Cease conceiving of education as mere preparation for later life, and make of it the full meaning of the present life.'" So educating through occupations does not mean teaching adult occupations as in much of vocational education. But then what exactly does it mean?

Key to understanding Dewey's sense of an education through occupations is that our lives are constituted by occupations. As we grow we take on new occupations, and these, as well as the occupations we have undertaken in the past, *are* who we are. Growing isn't a matter of learning about occupations that we may assume sometime in the future as adults; it isn't about acquiring knowledge we might apply down the track in an adult job. Instead, growing is about taking on occupations that – although historically formed – are significant to us at every phase of the life-course. In this way occupations can be understood as the evolving, building blocks of living. We grow into and *through* occupations throughout our lives. It is through the occupation we are living at any moment in time that we comprehend the people and environment around us – what they *mean*. In this way our occupations also enable us to understand other's perspectives, to see things in different ways. And they are the ways in which others understand us. For occupations are ways of being a person that sit within us, as who we are.

Additionally, our occupations orient our comprehension of future possibilities – opportunities and possibilities emerge from within current occupations. And these opportunities and possibilities offer potentially new occupations, new ways of being a person. We see chances for who we can be. So in this way we are always growing *through* occupations. We don't suddenly leap into occupations that have no connection with who we are.

Think of what it was like when you were entering your teenage years. This is not necessarily an easy task, but it is made easier when you are dealing directly with young people of this age and all they are going through. They are not the same as you are now; neither are younger children. One major way in which we differ is in relation to our interests. These shift and change as we grow – but as such, we grow *through* them, by way of them. Dewey understood that talking about interests in this way is the same as talking about occupations when these are understood aesthetically. We are talking about how we make *meaning*, why things are *significant* to us.

Importantly, such significance is never individualistic, as if an interest/occupation is something I decide upon in isolation of all other human beings. The significance of an occupation is social; occupations are always social callings. Even being a hermit on a mountaintop is a socially defined occupation. If it wasn't, no one else would have any conception of what a hermit does and knows. So the occupations that are significant to us at different times in our lives shift and change because of the social (and environmental) milieu in which we live. Who we are can never be separated from social and environmental context.

Dewey saw the organization of the school achieved via occupations (understood as units of work or projects), but not necessarily having generic forms across all schools. Thus he pointed out that "the types of activity remaining as true educative interests vary indefinitely with age, with individual native endowments, with prior experience, with social opportunities. It is out of the question to try to catalogue them" (1913, p. 67). But it is the teacher's responsibility to interpret and extend these interests into social occupations of significance. It is this idea that separated Dewey from progressives. "Interests in reality are but attitudes toward possible experiences," he wrote; "they are not achievements; their worth is in the leverage they afford, not in the accomplishment they represent" (1902b, p. 15). Such leverage is in the direction of doing and knowing – undertaking certain activities and learning relevant ideas. Interest as aesthetic experience is leveraged into the expenditure of effort as reflective experience. Occupations work across this important connection.

> The problem and the opportunity with the young is selection of orderly and continuous modes of occupation, which, while they lead up to and prepare for the indispensable activities of adult life, have their own *sufficient justification in their present reflex influence upon the formation of habits of thought.* (Dewey, 1933, p. 51)

Interest, when understood in its alignment with occupation, is aesthetic experience. Interest, as occupation, signals a way of being a person. But as most teachers (and parents) are very aware, we cannot simply impose a way of being on to young people and hope for resistance free compliance. Experience with trying to impose the occupation of being an academic student on to young people is an example of such a situation – one which requires an intricate classroom management and disciplinary structure to be able to enforce. In contrast, Dewey did not advocate for imposing occupations, but rather *discovering* them. He (1933, p. 52) believed that teachers would need to grapple with the problem of "discovering the valuable occupations," those occupations valued by a class group of young people (and also by their teacher, for different reasons). So this task of discovery is premised on the teacher's knowledge of the young people he or she is teaching. This is discovery of an occupation that leverages *their* interests.

Such discovery has been central to the progressive reforms that mark the historical development of education occurring out-of-doors. Nature study, school gardens, agricultural education and then school camping, blossoming into the many and various forms of outdoor education that Clifford Knapp describes such as conservation education, environmental education, adventure education and place-based education – all represent efforts made by teachers to discover occupations/interests held dear by the young people in their charge. And while each of these educational endeavors signals a move out-of-doors – a step through the doorway that marks the physical and metaphorical boundary of indoor education, of being an academic student – each is also a different occupation relevant in its historical context.

In this way Dewey's understanding of occupation illuminates, now with much more clarity, those definitions of outdoor education proffered by the Donaldsons and carried forward by others such as Ford that emphasize education *in, about* and *for* the outdoors. As mentioned previously, *in* the outdoors points to method, *about* the outdoors highlights subject matter, but now it can be seen that *for* the outdoors suggests an occupation when this is understood in terms of interest. Aesthetically, *for* intimates the holistic, immediate and direct connection we have with a way of being a person. Ford's comment below, while revealing the tension between method and subject matter in outdoor education, also illuminates aspects of the many occupations that have become part and parcel of outdoor education.

> To many people in the United States, Canada, England, and Australia, outdoor education is synonymous with education for outdoor pursuits or recreational skills. Snowshoeing, cross-country skiing, winter survival skills, backpacking, fishing, hunting, and related outdoor pursuits that are physical in nature (i.e. nonmechanized) and rely on the natural environment for implementation are the sole topics …. On the other hand, as many or more people feel that outdoor education is outdoor science education and consists only of teaching about natural resources and their interrelationship. Between the two poles of this spectrum are many people who seem to compromise on some, albeit weak, combination of the two issues. There are also those who would not agree with either point of view, because they feel that outdoor education is not a separate subject, but rather a process of teaching (any subject) in the outdoors. (Ford, 1981, p. 69)

For the 'outdoors' can thus manifest in a myriad of ways, each connecting with an occupation as interest. It is the work of the teacher to discover the *for* that can garner the interest of the young people involved. This can be expressed as the teacher's *feel* for the lives of these young people, a feel for their interests. It points to the importance of comprehending *their* social worlds, understanding who they are.

But outdoor education through occupations involves more than just *for*, as interest. Education *in* the outdoors points to doing, to method, to "continuous activity having a purpose" (Dewey 1916a, p. 361). Education *about* the outdoors highlights knowing subject matter, but this always within an occupation that acts as "an organizing principle for information and ideas; for knowledge and intellectual growth" (p. 362). So the task of the teacher does not end with discovering an occupation as interest. In a reflective planning sense the teacher is involved in "arranging" (1933, p. 52) the occupation. Such arranging includes what we normally think of as teacher's work: arranging curriculum and pedagogy, subject matter and method, content and process, knowing and doing, what and how. This means making decisions regarding *in* and *about* as these connect with *for*. This tells us that in our reflective arranging, we are also influencing how the occupation will be experienced aesthetically. When we change our teaching arrangements, we know this will change the way the experience feels.

An occupation concerns being a certain type of person, which involves doing certain tasks, and knowing certain facts/knowledge. It is the teacher's work to bring all three aspects together. This does not mean prioritising any one above the others, but addressing all three.

As such, education *in*, *about* and *for* the 'outdoors' are not in conflict with each other. Rather, each is a necessary aspect of education, as revealed in Dewey's identification of two types of reflective experience (doing and knowing) and aesthetic experience (being). Each is necessary because each is a mode of experience.

Outdoor education programs are thus designed by way of occupations. One key advantage of outdoor education is that it allows teachers to discover and arrange occupations beyond the bounds of the many constraints that hamper indoor education. The many possible occupations that come under the banner of outdoor education are often embraced by young people as significant to them and their future; however they can always be improved. As outdoor educators we need to be more aware of how the programs we design, via the methods and subject matter that we engage with, can be improved by a Deweyan understanding of education *through* occupations – as can all education, without any prefixes attached.

Taking such a view to education more broadly, and not just outdoor education (prefixed), is revealed in Dewey's trinity of the school as "(1) the life of the school as a social institution in itself; (2) methods of learning and of doing work; and (3) the school studies or curriculum" (1909, p. 29). Occupations connect with life, they suggest the methods as activities and they structure the meaning of the curriculum. Yet the official and primary occupation of schooling is being an academic student. How does the school connect with life if this is the case? By conceiving of education as preparation for a future adult existence. But is this a true connection with life? We believe that Dewey has argued against such an educational situation. So how could we alternatively organize the life of the school?

This is a question that has engaged educators for more than a century, reflected in the many attempts at reform that have characterized the educational situation, resulting in conflict, confusion and compromise. But as yet none of these reforms has provided a way out, a way forward beyond such tensions. Instead they have simply complicated the situation further because they remain ensconced in the method and subject matter debate. Getting to a level deeper was the challenge that Dewey presented to himself and to us. He gave us a direction to follow: understand ourselves, our experience, it's existential and historical dimensions – and then we shall better understand what education *is*. We hope we have shed some light on this path, however we leave you to ponder its further significance and the many ramifications for the future of outdoor education – and for education in general.

NOTE

[1] Contemporary educational scholar Alexander Sidorkin (2010) has argued that schools are involved in what he calls "the wastebasket economy," where children are essentially conscripted into producing marks on pieces of paper with no value to anyone. There, "learning is a byproduct of making useless things," he provocatively argues.

REFERENCES

Adams, A., & Reynolds, S. (1981). The long conversation: Tracing the roots of the past. *Journal of Experiential Education. 4*(1), 21–28.

Apple, M., Au, W., & Gandin, L.A. (Eds.) (2009). *The Routledge International Handbook of Critical Education.* New York: Routledge.

Armstrong, C.F. (1990). The making of good men: Character-building in the New England boarding schools. In P.W. Kingston & L.S. Lewis (Eds.), *The high-status track: Studies of elite schools and social stratification* (pp. 3–24). Albany, NY: SUNY Press.

Bailey, L.H. (1903). *The nature-study idea.* New York: Doubleday, Page & Company.

Beach, K. (1995). Sociocultural change, activity, and individual development: Some methodological aspects. *Mind. Culture and Activity. 2*(4), 277–284.

Blackman, C.A. (1969). Perspective: A curriculum specialist looks at outdoor education. *Journal of Outdoor Education. 3*(3), 3–5.

Boud, D., Keogh, R., & Walker, D. (1985). What is reflection in learning? In D. Boud, R. Keough & D. Walker, *Reflection: Turning experience into learning* (pp. 7–17). Oxon: Routledge.

Bowers, C.A. (2005). *The false promises of constructivist learning theories: A global and ecological critique.* New York: Peter Lang Publishing.

Breunig, M. (2011). Paulo Freire: Critical praxis and experiential education. In T.E. Smith & C.E. Knapp (Eds.). *Sourcebook of experiential education: Key thinkers and their contributions.* New York: Routledge.

Brookes, A. (2002). Lost in the Australian bush: Outdoor education as curriculum. *Journal of Curriculum Studies. 34*(4), 405–425.

Carlson, R.E. (1947). School camping is on the way. *The Physical Educator. 5*(1), 8–26.

Coleman, J. (1995). Experiential learning and information processing: Toward an appropriate mix. In K. Warren, M. Sakofs & J. Hunt (Eds.), *The Theory of Experiential Education* (pp. 123–130). Dubuque, IA: Kendall Hunt.

Comstock, A.B. (1911). *Handbook of nature-study for teachers and parents.* Ithaca, NY: The Comstock Publishing Company.

Comstock, A.B. (1915). The growth and influence of the nature-study idea. *The Nature-Study Review. 11*(1), 5–11.

Cooper, G. (2005). Disconnected children. *Ecos. 26*(1), 26–31.

Counts, G.S. (1932). *Dare the school build a new social order?* New York: The John Day Company.

Curtis, E.W. (1909). Out-door schools. *The Pedagogical Seminary. 16*(2), 169–194.

Dewey, J. (1893). Self-realization as the moral ideal. *The Philosophical Review. 2*(6), 652–664.

Dewey, J. (1896). The influence of the high school upon educational methods. *The School Review. 4*(1), 1–12.

Dewey, J. (1897a). My pedagogic creed. *The School Journal. 54*(January), 77–80.

Dewey, J. (1897b). The psychological aspect of the school curriculum. *Educational Review. 13*(April), 356–369.

Dewey, J. (1900). *The school and society.* Chicago: The University of Chicago Press.

Dewey J. (1902a). *The educational situation.* Chicago: The University of Chicago Press.

Dewey, J. (1902b). *The child and the curriculum.* Chicago: The University of Chicago Press.

Dewey, J. (1903). Thought and its subject-matter: The general problem of logical theory. In J. Dewey (Ed.), *Studies in logical theory* (pp. 1–22). Chicago: The University of Chicago Press.

Dewey, J. (1909). *The moral principles in education.* Boston, MA: Houghton Mifflin & Co.

Dewey, J. (1911). Education. In P. Monroe (Ed.), *A cyclopedia of education. Vol. II* (pp. 398–401). New York: Macmillan.

Dewey, J. (1913). *Interest and effort in education.* Cambridge, MA: The Riverside Press.

Dewey, J. (1915). *The school and society* (2nd rev ed.). Chicago: University of Chicago Press.

Dewey, J. (1916a). *Democracy and education.* New York: The Free Press.

REFERENCES

Dewey, J. (1916b). *Essays in experimental logic*. New York: Dover Publications.

Dewey, J. (1926). Affective thought. *Journal of the Barnes Foundation, 2*(April), 3–9.

Dewey, J. (1929a). *Experience and nature* (2nd ed.). Chicago: Open Court Publishing Company.

Dewey, J. (1929b). *The quest for certainty: A study of the relation of knowledge and action*. New York: Minton, Balch and Company.

Dewey, J. (1930). Qualitative thought. *Symposium, 1*(January), 5–32.

Dewey, J. (1931). *The way out of educational confusion*. Cambridge, MA: Harvard University Press.

Dewey, J. (1933). *How we think: A restatement of the relation of reflective thinking to the educative process* (rev ed.). Boston: D.C. Heath and Company.

Dewey, J. (1934a). *Art as experience*. New York: Capricorn Books.

Dewey, J. (1934b). Why I am not a communist. *Modern Monthly, 8*(April), 135–137.

Dewey, J. (1935). The need for orientation. *Forum, 93*(June), 333–335.

Dewey, J. (1938). *Experience and education*. New York: Collier Books.

Dewey, J. (1939). Experience, knowledge and value: A rejoinder. In P.A. Schilpp (Ed.), *The philosophy of John Dewey* (pp. 515–608). Evanston, IL: Northwestern University Press.

Dewey, J., & Childs, J.L. (1933). The underlying philosophy of education. In W.H. Kilpatrick (Ed.). *The educational frontier*. New York: D. Appleton-Century Company.

Dewey, J., & Dewey, E. (1915). *Schools of tomorrow*. New York: E.P. Dutton & Co.

Dimock, H.S., & Hendry, C.S. (1929). *Camping and character: A camp experiment in character education*. New York: Association Press.

Donaldson, G., & Donaldson, L. (1958). Outdoor education: A definition. *Journal of Health, Physical Education & Recreation, 29*(May), 17–63.

Donaldson, G.W. (1972). Research in outdoor education. *Journal of Environmental Education, 3*(4), 9–10.

Eckert, P. (1989). *Jocks and burnouts: Social categories and identity in the high school*. New York: Teachers College Press.

Eells, E. (1986). *Eleanor Eell's history of organized camping: The first 100 years*. Martinsville, IN: American Camping Association.

Fallace, T. (2012). Race, culture and pluralism: The evolution of Dewey's vision for a democratic curriculum. *Journal of Curriculum Studies, 44*(1), 13–35.

Ford, P. (1981). *Principles and practices of outdoor/environmental education*. New York: John Wiley & Sons.

Freeman, M. (2011). From 'character-training' to 'personal growth': The early history of Outward Bound 1941–1965. *History of Education, 40*(1), 21–43.

Gager, R. (1977). As a learning process … it's more than just getting your hands dirty. *Voyageur, 1*.

Garvey, D. (1990). A history of the AEE. In J.C. Miles & S. Priest (Eds.), *Adventure education* (pp. 75–82). State College, PA: Venture Publishing.

Gibson, H.W. (1936). The history of organized camping: the early days. *The Camping Magazine, 8*(January), 13–15, 26–28.

Greenberg, E. (1978). The community as a learning resource. *Journal of Experiential Education, 1*(2), 22–25.

Gruenewald, D.A. (2003a). The best of both worlds: A critical pedagogy of place. *Educational Researcher, 32*(4), 3–12.

Gruenewald, D.A. (2003b). Foundations of place: A multidisciplinary framework for place-conscious education. *American Educational Research Journal, 40*(3), 619–654.

Gruenewald, D.A. (2005). Accountability and collaboration: Institutional barriers and strategic pathways for place-based education. *Ethics, Place & Environment, 8*(3), 261–283.

Hahn, K. (1957). Origins of the outward bound trust. In D. James (Ed.), *Outward bound*. London: Routledge and Kegan Paul.

Haluza-DeLay, R. (2001). Nothing here to care about: Participant constructions of nature following a 12-day wilderness program. *The Journal of Environmental Education, 32*(4), 43–48.

Hammerman, W.M. (1980). Epilogue. In W.M. Hammerman (Ed.), *Fifty years of resident outdoor education: 1930–1980* (pp. 125–127). Martinsville, IN: American Camping Association.

Hanks, W.F. (1991). Foreword. In J. Lave & E. Wenger. *Situated learning: Legitimate peripheral participation*. Cambridge, UK: Cambridge University Press.

Higgins, C. (2005). Dewey's conception of vocation: Existential, aesthetic, and educational implications for teachers. *Journal of Curriculum Studies. 37*(4), 441–464.

Horwood, B. (1989). Reflections on reflection. *Journal of Experiential Education. 12*(2), 5–9.

Jackman, W. (1891). *Nature study for the common schools.* New York: Henry Holt & Co.

Jennings, N., Swidler, S., & Koliba, C. (2005). Place-based education in the standards-based reform era: Conflict or complement? *American Journal of Education. 112*(1), 44–65.

Joplin, L. (1981). On defining experiential education. *Journal of Experiential Education, 4*(1), 17–20.

Kaestle, C.F. (1983). *Pillars of the republic: Common schools and American society 1780–1860.* New York: Hill & Wang.

Katz, R., & Kolb, D. (1968). *Outward Bound as education for personal growth.* Cambridge, MA: Massachusetts Institute of Technology.

Keeton, M. (1976). Credentials for a learning society. In M. Keeton (Ed.), *Experiential learning: Rationale. characteristics. assessment* (pp. 1–18). San Francisco: Jossey-Bass Publishers.

Kilpatrick, W.H. (1929). Foreword. In H.S. Dimock & C.S. Hendry, *Camping and character: A camp experiment in character education* (pp. vii–xi). New York: Association Press.

Kilpatrick, W.H. (1942). The role of camping in education today. *The Camping Magazine. 14*(February), 14–16.

Kirk, J. (1975). Outdoor education, conservation education: a quantum jump. *Journal of Outdoor Education. 9*(2), 2–8.

Kliebard, H.M. (2004). *The struggle for the American curriculum: 1893–1958* (3rd ed.). New York: Routledge.

Knapp, C.E. (1967). Some challenges in outdoor education. *Journal of Outdoor Education. 2*(1), 8–9, 10–12.

Knapp, C.E. (1997). Environmental and outdoor education for the 21st century. *Taproot, 10*(4), 3–9.

Kolb, D.A. (1984). *Experiential learning: Experience as the source of learning and development.* Upper Saddle River, NJ: Prentice Hall.

Koschmann, T., Kuutti, K., & Hickman, L. (1998). The concept of breakdown in Heidegger, Leont'ev, and Dewey and its implications for education. *Mind. Culture, and Activity. 5*(1), 25–41.

Kraft, R.J. (1985). Towards a theory of experiential learning. In R.J. Kraft (Ed.), *The theory of experiential education* (2nd ed.) (pp. 7–38). Boulder, CO: Association for Experiential Education.

Laszlo, E. (1972). The new concept of the environment. *The Journal of Environmental Education. 3*(3). 14–18.

Lewis, C. (1975). *The administration of outdoor education programs.* Dubuque, IO: Kendall Hunt Publishing.

Lieberman, J. (1932). What is a progressive camp? *Association Boys' Work Journal. 5*(4), 9–11.

Louv, R. (2008). *Last child in the woods: Saving our children from nature-deficit disorder* (updated and expanded ed.). Chapel Hill, NC: Algonquin Books of Chapel Hill.

Lucas, A.M. (1972). Environment and environmental education: Conceptual issues and curriculum implications. *Dissertation Abstracts International. 33*(11), 6064. (UMI No. 7311531)

Lucas, A.M. (1979). *Environment and environmental education: Conceptual issues and curriculum implications.* Kew, AUS: Australian International Press & Publications.

Mason, B.S. (1930). *Camping and education.* New York: The McCall Company.

McEvoy III, J. (1972). The American concern with environment. In W. Burch, N. Cheek, & L. Taylor (Eds.), *Social behavior. natural resources. and the environment* (pp. 214–236). New York: Harper & Row.

Meyers, I.B. (1910). The evolution of aim and method in the teaching of nature-study in the common schools of the united states. *The Elementary School Teacher. 11*(4), 205–213.

Meyers, I.B. (1911). The evolution of aim and method in the teaching of nature-study in the common schools of the United States (concluded). *The Elementary School Teacher. 11*(5), 237–248.

Michelson, E. (1999). Carnival, paranoia, and experiential learning. *Studies in the Education of Adults. 31*(2), 140–154.

Miettinen, R. (2000). The concept of experiential learning and John Dewey's theory of reflective thought and action. *International Journal of Lifelong Education. 19*(1), 54–72.

Miettinen, R. (2006). Epistemology of transformative material activity: John Dewey's pragmatism and cultural-historical activity theory. *Journal for the Theory of Social Behavior. 36*(4), 389–407.

REFERENCES

Miles, J.C., & Priest, S. (1990). *Adventure education*. State College, PA: Venture Publishing.

Millikan, M. (2006). The muscular Christian ethos in post-second world war American Liberalism: Women in Outward Bound 1962–1975. *The International Journal of the History of Sport, 23*(5), 838–855.

Miner, J.L., & Bolt, J. (1981). *Outward Bound U.S.A.: Learning through experience in adventure-based education*. New York: William Morrow and Company.

Minton, T.G. (1980). The history of the nature-study movement and its role in the development of environmental education. *Dissertation Abstracts International, 41*(03), 967. (UMI No. 8019480)

Mitchell, D.O. (1923). A history of nature-study. *The Nature-Study Review, 19*, 258–274 & 295–321.

Mitchell, E.D. (1938). The interests of education in camping. *Phi Delta Kappan, 24*(1), 140–142.

Mueller, M.P. (2009). Educational reflections on the 'ecological crisis': EcoJustice, environmentalism, and sustainability. *Science and Education, 18*(8), 1031–1056.

Orr, D. (2002). Political economy and the ecology of childhood. In P.H. Kahn & S.R. Kellert (Eds.), *Children and Nature: Psychological, Sociocultural, and Evolutionary Investigations* (pp. 279–303). Cambridge, MA: MIT Press.

Paris, L. (2008). *Children's nature: The rise of the American summer camp*. New York: New York University Press.

Patterson, A.J. (1921). A survey of twenty years" progress made in the courses of nature study. *Nature-Study Review, 17*(2), 55–62.

Petzoldt, P. (1974). *The wilderness handbook*. New York: W.W. Norton and Company.

Popkewitz, T.S. (2007). Alchemies and governing: Or, questions about the questions we ask. *Educational Philosophy and Theory, 39*(1), 64–83.

Priest, S. (1986). Redefining outdoor education: A matter of many relationships. *Journal of Environmental Education, 17*(3), 13–15.

Priest, S., & Gass, M. (1997). *Effective leadership in adventure programming*. Champaign, IL: Human Kinetics.

Pyle, R.M. (2001). The rise and fall of natural history: How a science grew that eclipsed direct experience. *Orion, 4*, 16–23.

Quay, J. (in press). More than relations between self, others and nature: Outdoor education and aesthetic experience. *Journal of Adventure Education and Outdoor Learning*.

Ready, M.M. (1933). *Camps and public schools* (Office of Education Circular Number 74). Washington, DC: United States Department of the Interior.

Rice, W.M. (1888). Science teaching in the schools (continued). *The American Naturalist, 22*(262), 897–913.

Roberts, J. (2012). *Beyond learning by doing: Theoretical currents in experiential education*. New York: Routledge.

Säljö, R., & Wyndhamm, J. (1993). The school as a context for problem solving. In S. Chaiklin & J. Lave (Eds.), *Understanding practice: Perspectives on activity and context* (pp. 327–342). Cambridge: Cambridge University Press.

Sargent, P. (1926). *A Handbook of Summer Camps* (3rd ed.). Boston: Porter Sargent.

School Garden Association of America. (1916). *Outdoor Education, 1*(1).

Seaman, J. (2008). Experience, reflect, critique: The end of the "learning cycles" era. In K. Warren, D. Mitten & T. Loeffler (Eds.), *Theory and Practice of Experiential Education* (pp. 223–236). Boulder, CO: Association for Experiential Education.

Seaman, J., & Rheingold, A. (2012). Selling out or buying in? Imperatives for outdoor education in the age of accountability. In B. Martin & M. Wagstaff (Eds.), *Controversial issues in adventure programming* (pp. 258–264). Champaign, IL: Human Kinetics.

Sharp, L.B. (1930). *Education and the summer camp: An experiment*. New York: Teachers College Columbia University.

Sharp, L.B. (1943). Outside the classroom. *The Educational Forum, 7*(4), 361–368.

Sharp, L.B. (1947). Basic considerations in outdoor and camping education. *The Bulletin of the National Association of Secondary School Principals, 31*(147), 43–48.

Sharp, L.B. (1948). Why outdoor and camping education? *Journal of Educational Sociology, 21*(5), 313–318.

Sharp, L.B. (1952). What is outdoor education? *The School Executive, 71*, 19–22.

Sharp, L.B., & Osborne, E.G. (1940). Schools and camping: A review of recent developments. *Progressive Education, 17*(4), 236–241.

Shore, A., & Greenberg, E. (1978). Challenging the past, present, & future: New directions in education. *Journal of Experiential Education, 1*(1), 42–46.

Sidorkin, A. (2010). *Labor of learning: Market and the next generation of educational reform.* Rotterdam: Sense Publishers.

Smith, G.A. (2002). Place-based education: Learning to be where we are. *Phi Delta Kappan, 83*(April), 584–594.

Smith, G.A. (2007). Place-based education: Breaking through the constraining regularities of public school. *Environmental Education Research. 13*(2), 189–207.

Smith, J.W. (1960). The scope of outdoor education. *Bulletin of the National Association of Secondary School Principals, 44*, 156–158.

Smith, J.W. (1966). A decade of progress in outdoor education. *Journal of Outdoor Education. 1*(1), 3–5.

Smith, J.W. (1970). Where we have been – what we are – what we will become. *Journal of Outdoor Education. 5*(1), 3–7.

Smith, J.W., Carlson, R.E., Donaldson, G.W., & Masters, H.B. (1972). *Outdoor education* (2nd ed.). Englewood Cliffs, NJ: Prentice-Hall.

Stapp, W.B. (1974). Historical setting of environmental education. In J. Swan & W. Stapp (Eds.), *Environmental education: Strategies toward a more livable future* (pp. 42–49). New York: John Wiley & Sons.

Strong, E.A. (1889). Shall we teach geology? *Science. 13*(322), 269.

Swett, J. (1900). *American public schools: History and pedagogics.* New York: American Book Company.

Thoreau, H.D. (2001). *Henry David Thoreau: Collected essays and poems.* New York: Library of America.

Twining, H.H. (1938). The functional program of the American Camping Association. *Phi Delta Kappan. 21*(4), 137–139.

Tyack, D., & Cuban, L. (1995) *Tinkering toward utopia: A century of public school reform.* Cambridge, MA: Harvard University Press.

Upton, S.M.H. (1914). Open-air schools. *Teachers College Record. 15*(3).

Vinal, W.G. (1922). The summer camp and nature-study. *The Nature-Study Review. 18*(4), 113–118.

Vinal, W.G. (1926). *Nature guiding.* Ithaca, NY: The Comstock Publishing Co.

Vinal, W.G. (1936). The school camp line-up for nature education. *The Clearing House, 10*, 462–466.

Vinal, W.G. (1940). *Nature recreation. Group guidance for the out-of-doors.* New York: McGraw-Hill Book Company.

Vinal, W.G. (1974–75). The growth of the concept of nature recreation. *Nature Study. 28*(4), 1–8.

Vokey, D. (1987). *Outward Bound: In search of foundations.* Unpublished masters thesis, Queen's University at Kingston, Ontario, Canada.

Ward, C.E. (1935). *Organized camping and progressive education.* Nashville, TN: Cullom & Ghertner Company.

Walsh, V. & Golins, G.L. (1976). *The exploration of the outward bound process.* Denver, CO: Colorado Outward Bound School. (ERIC Document Reproduction Service No. ED144754)

Wells, G., & Claxton, G. (2002). *Learning for life in the 21st century.* Oxford, UK: Blackwell Publishers.

Westbrook, R.B. (1991). *John Dewey and American democracy.* Ithaca, NY: Cornell University Press.

White House Conference on Child Health and Protection. (1933). *Summer Vacation Activities of the School Child.* New York: The Century Company.

Willis, P.E. (1977). *Learning to labour: How working class kids get working class jobs.* Farnborough, UK: Saxon House.

Wichmann, T.F. (1980). Babies and bath water: Two experiential heresies. *Journal of Experiential Education. 3*(1), 6–12.

Wiener, M. (1967). Outdoor education can help unlock the school. *Educational Leadership. 24*(8), 696–699.

Wilson, W. (1977). Social discontent and the growth of wilderness sport in America: 1965–1974. *Quest. 27*, 54–60.

REFERENCES

Woodhouse, J.L., & Knapp, C.E. (2000). *Place-based curriculum and instruction: Outdoor and environmental education approaches.* Charleston WV: ERIC Clearinghouse on Rural Education and Small Schools. (ERIC Document Reproduction Service No. ED448012)

Wurdinger, S., & Paxton, T. (2003). Using multiple levels of experience to promote autonomy in adventure education students. *Journal of Adventure Education & Outdoor Learning, 3*(1), 41–48.

Zajchowski, R.A. (1978). The establishment critics: A summary of the major reports on secondary education in the 1970s. *Journal of Experiential Education, 1*(2), 5–12.

Zook, L.R. (1986). Outdoor adventure programs build character five ways. *Parks & Recreation, 21*(January), 54–57.

Zueblin, C. (1916). *American municipal progress.* New York: Macmillan.

ABOUT THE AUTHORS

John Quay BEd, GradDipEdAdmin, PGradDipEdStudies (Student Wellbeing), MEd, PhD
Senior Lecturer
Graduate School of Education
The University of Melbourne

John spent numerous years working as an outdoor education teacher with students in secondary schools. These experiences led him to question where outdoor education had come from and its place within education more generally. Seeking answers to these questions resulted in making the transition to an academic career and a keen interest in the work of John Dewey.

Jayson Seaman, BS (English Teaching), MS (Outdoor Education), PhD (Experiential Education)
Associate Professor, Department of Kinesiology
Affiliate Faculty, Department of Education
University of New Hampshire

Jayson began his career as a youth professional at 17, when he was a summer camp counsellor. He subsequently served various roles in public schooling, from a classroom English teacher to a district-wide experiential program coordinator to a State and federal grants manager, working in the K-12 Learn and Serve program during the Clinton era. He is continuously struck by how acutely John Dewey understood deep and persistent educational problems, and remains committed to supporting initiatives in and out of school that approximate Dewey's innovative solutions.

Printed in the United States
By Bookmasters